SCOTCH - IRISH FAMILY RESEARCH MADE SIMPLE

by
R. G. CAMPBELL

SUMMIT PUBLICATIONS
NOW PUBLISHED BY
YE OLDE GENEALOGIE SHOPPE
PO BOX 39128
INDIANAPOLIS, IN 46239

ISBN 1-878311-14-X

SCOTCH-IRISH FAMILY RESEARCH MADE SIMPLE

INTRODUCTION TO THE REVISED EDITION (1992)

Scotch-Irish Family Research Made Simple was first published in 1974. Revised Editions were published in 1982 and in 1987. These editions considerably expanded the information in chapters III and IV. Now, again in 1992, some material is being added and other material is being revised.

As one reads the history of the immigrants to the United States, it becomes clear that the 18th Century immigrants from Ulster were different people than those Irish, principally from the South and West, who fled famine and persecution, to come to America in the 19th Century. Our series of family research publications, therefore, treats these two different peoples in separate books. The history and the migration of the people of the South of Ireland is covered in E. J. Collins work, "Irish Family Research Made Simple". This book is intended to supplement that by covering the "Irish of the North" or as we have come to know them, "the Scotch-Irish".

LIST OF ILLUSTRATIONS

Figure

CHAPTER I

THE SCOTS MIGRATE TO ULSTER - A BRIEF HISTORY

The story of the Scotch-Irish in America really starts about 1600, just before the Scottish King James VI became King James I of the United Kingdom. As James I he would make land grants in the northern part of Ireland to Scottish landlords and English merchants. Those who received the land would not necessarily go to Ireland themselves, but were to get their tenants and others to migrate to the northern Irish Province of Ulster.(Northern Ireland, the political entity that we know in 1987 is not identical to the historic Province of Ulster. More on this in Chapter IV.) It was hoped that these new settlers would establish farms and thereby secure the area for England.

In 1600 Scotland was a land of poverty and insecurity.Its past had known very few times of peace. There had been constant war with England. No King of Scotland, since Robert the Bruce in 1300, had been able to keep the English out. Five of the kings, between 1400 and 1625 were minors. The succession of regencies gave the nobles plenty of opportunities to eliminate the royal control. When King James became both King of Scotland and King of England in 1603, upon the death of Queen Elizabeth I, he was able, at last, to establish peace along the Scottish-English border. In fact, he brought peace to most of the Lowlands of Scotland. The Highlands had not yet achieved anywhere near the civilized life of the Lowlanders. The Highlanders lived in a desolate region and derived much of their livelihood from raids on the Lowland towns and farms.

At about this time religious fervor in Scotland, at least in the Lowlands, was at fever pitch. Religion was a primary reason for part of the migration to Ireland and it gave the Scotch-Ulster immigrants a distinctive character that they never lost, not even after later migration from Ulster to America. Scotland became Christianized in the 6th Century. The Scots were converted primarily by an Irish monk, St. Cuthbert. The Church did not flourish in Scotland until about the 12th Century. From then until about 1560 the Roman Church was well established.Scotland was not touched by the many religious movements and enthusiasms which had touched other parts of Europe during this period. At a time when saints were common in other areas, Scotland had no saints. When scholars, such as Thomas Aquinas and others, were flourishing abroad, Scotland had no scholars. Scotland remained on the fringes of Christianity. By the middle of the 16th Century, the Church was in a lamentable condition, even more so than in many other countries of Europe.

When the Protestant Reformation was sweeping across Europe, Scotland was touched very little. Some historians conclude that the Reformation might never have touched Scotland, had it not been for the greed of the noblemen, and that the Scottish Reformation actually began as a political movement. It is unlikely that the Reformation in any country in Europe was entirely religious in its motivation. It was with the return of John Knox from exile in 1599 that the Reformation took fire in Scotland. A religious-civil war took place which lasted about a year. In 1560 the Parliament put an end to the Church of Rome as the National Church of Scotland. By 1561 the Presbyterian Church was established as the "Kirk of Scotland".

Throughout the five centuries since the Norman King Henry II had sent "Strongbow", the Earl of Pembrooke, to invade Ireland, the English continually and unsuccessfully tried to subdue the Irish. The English kings, after each successful Irish campaign, gave land in Ireland to Anglo-Norman families. They had hoped that by having the Englishmen settle in Ireland, they would spread the English influence and that eventually the island would be totally held by the Englishmen for the Crown. However, it never worked out quite that way. Before many years, the Anglo-Normans inter-married with the Irish and soon, as some historians say, became more Irish than the Irish themselves. Only a small area around Dublin, called "the Pale", was really securely English. By the time of the English Queen Elizabeth I, the fighting was no longer sporadic, but was a constant drain on the royal treasury. In Elizabeth's day, Ulster, the northern province of Ireland, was not distinguishable from the other parts of the island. It was the same as Munster in the southwest, Connaught in the west and Leinster in the east. It was the same as these provinces in its language, religion, poverty and hatred of the English.

The Reformation never came to Ireland. No Luther, Knox or Calvin arose, and the Church of England, though well established in the Pale, had made no real attempt to win the people of Ulster, or of any part of the island, at that time. On the other hand, the Jesuits chose Ireland as one of their main centers of missionary activity, for the work of the Counter-Reformation. They did their work well, so well that three-fourths of the people of the south of Ireland are still Catholic.

While none of Ireland was peaceful, the English had their worst trouble in the northern Province of Ulster. There, the greatest of the clan leaders, the O'Neil, Tyreconnel and O'Cahane, were constantly fighting the English. Queen Elizabeth I had even tried to win over the O'Neil by bestowing upon him the Earldom of Tyronne. In 1595 the Irish Chiefs led a great rebellion against the English. Lord Essex, who commanded the

English troops, could not subdue the Irish. Elizabeth then sent Lord Mountjoy to replace Essex. He was able to defeat Tyronne (the O'Neil) only by destroying all of the houses, food and cattle in the region. The depopulation of the region due to the war, made a new plantation scheme in Ulster appear very feasible.

After Elizabeth's death, the new King James I of England(King James VI of Scotland) followed up on the plantation scheme. Initially James' advisors had envisioned primarily just another plantation of English colonists, and many did emigrate from the English countryside and London to Ulster. These settled primarily in Counties Armagh and Coleraine, which name the English changed to Londonderry, and eventually to just Derry. Scottish participation did not originally seem important to James' advisors, but the Scots were eventually to become the mainstay of the plantation. James made great grants of land to the Earl of Abecorn and the Duke of Lennox, both Scottish noblemen. He made other grants to other of the great barons of the Lowland Counties of Southwestern Scotland.

The map in Figure 1 shows the counties of Scotland and distinguishes which are considered Lowland and which are Highland. The emigrants to Ulster came from the Lowland and border counties. James knew the adventurous nature of the Scots, the poverty of Scotland, and the appeal to them of a good bargain. The assignment of land in Ulster to the Scots had a permanent effect on the character of that part of Ireland.

Those counties planted primarily with Scots continued to show a predominance of Presbyterianism, while those settled by the Englishmen were normally those in which the Church of England flourished. Counties Donegal and Tyronne were heavily settled by Scots; Armagh and Derry, as previously mentioned, were heavily settled by the English. Fermagh and Cavan were heavily settled by both, including many people from the borderlands. Such border names as Armstrong, Elliot and Beatty appeared frequently among the settlers. Down and Antrim had some settlers from both Scotland and England. Those from Scotland who settled in Down and Antrim, came primarily from the Scottish counties of Ayr, Renfrew, Wigton and Lanark. They included such names asJohnston, Kennedy, Scott, Maxwell, Gibson, Dixon, McKee, Hamilton and Campbell. Only Monaghan, of the nine counties of Ulster, remained truly Irish, for only one successful settlement was made there. When in 1922, the Irish Free State was formed, later to become the Republic of Ireland, three counties of Ulster, namely Monaghan, Cavan and Donegal, joined the Free State, while the other six counties became what we know today as Northern Ireland. The map in Figure 2 shows the counties of Ulster, with an additional heavy line

THE SCOTTISH HIGHLANDS AND LOWLANDS

FIG. 1

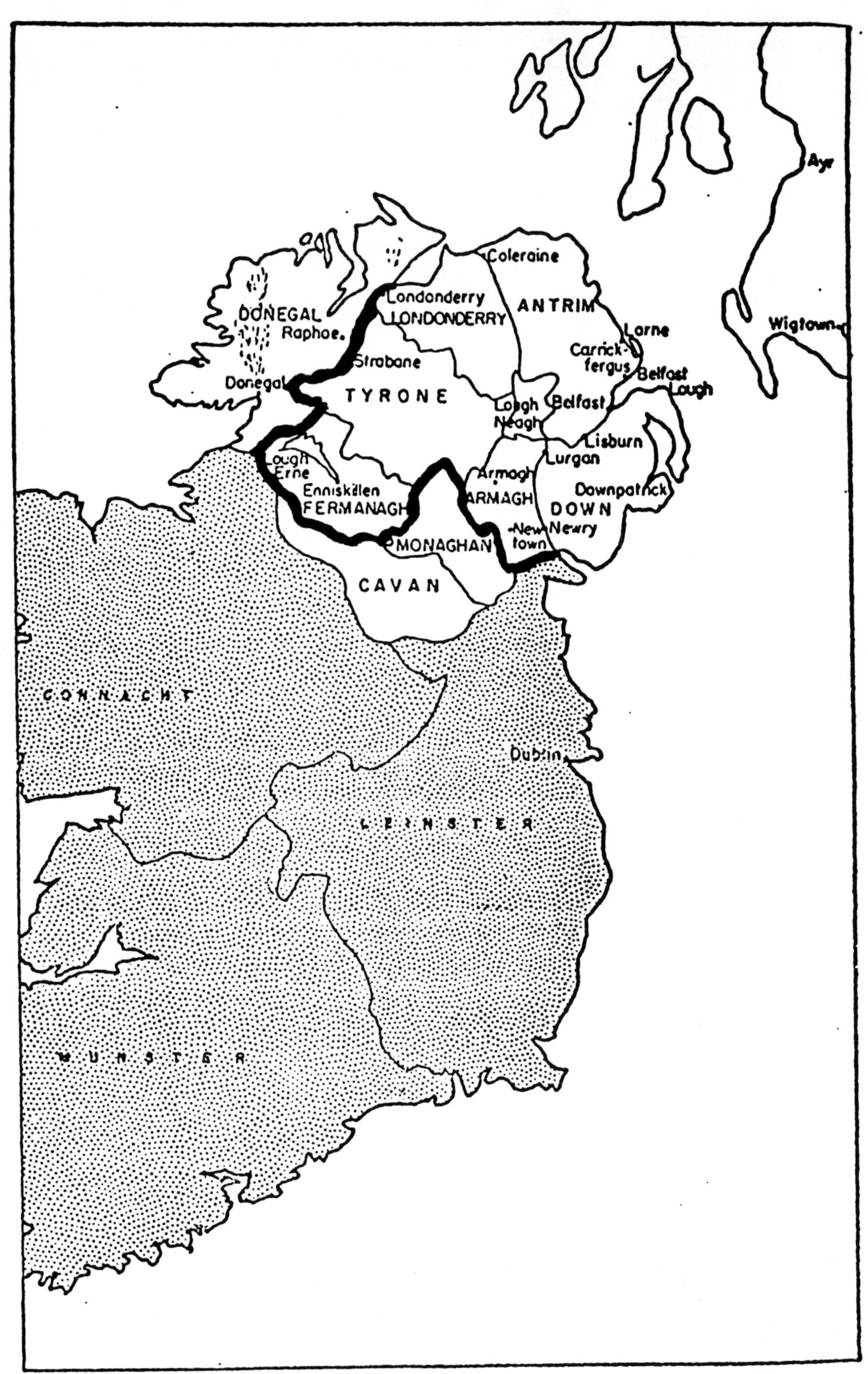

NORTHERN IRELAND AND ULSTER

FIG. 2

indicating the present border between the Republic of Ireland and Northern Ireland.

There are several good books concerning details of the various plantations in Ulster. "An Historic Account of the Plantation of Ulster, 1608-1620", by George Hill was written in 1877, but has recently been reprinted by Irish University Press. Another, "The Londonderry Plantation", by T.W. Moody is out of print at present but copies may sometimes be obtained in Irish bookshops (see Chapter IV). Another, and more recently published book is "The Scottish Migration to Ulster in the Reign of James I", by M. Percival Maxwell. This, too, was published in Ireland.

The main attraction of Ulster for the Scots in the early 1600's was the hope of a better economic future. They wanted to escape the grinding poverty of 17th Century Scotland. Later a second reason was added. They wanted to be free of the violence which took place in Scotland during the reign of Charles I and Richard Cromwell. Each of these had taken repressive measures against the Kirk of Scotland(Presbyterian). Principally, they tried to change the form of government of the Presbyterian Church to make it conform to one more like that of the Established Church of England. While this was occurring in Scotland, there was comparative freedom of worship in Ulster, so thousands of Scots emigrated. The emigration from the Lowlands of Scotland to Ulster continued throughout most of the 17th Century.

The first of the Scots to come to Ireland (Ulster) in the first decade of the 17th Century (1600-1610) were, according to the standard histories, some of the lowest classes in Scotland. They probably were not as bad as they were painted by the Reverend Andrew Stewart, a Presbyterian minister in the County Down, who referred to the early immigrants as "the scum of both Scotland and England". They probably were, in fact, no worse than the immigrants who left England for Virginia, or the Scots who left Scotland for Russia or France in earlier centuries. The immigrants must have been the right kind of people for the job to be done, since they gave Ulster a reputation that was to attract others in the 1630's and later. No doubt this later immigration did represent a larger proportion of higher types of people. But as a later Scotch poet, Robert Burns, observed, "rank is but a tinsel show". It was during this later period that the ministers arrived in goodly numbers and firmly planted the Presbyterian Church in Ulster. The emigration from Scotland continued throughout most of the 17th Century and was heaviest near the end of the century.

In 1689 when William of Orange ascended the throne of England, the Scots achieved freedom to practice their religion, and when in 1707, the Act of Union brought Scotland and England together into the United Kingdom, the economic condition of the Lowlands of Scotland became vastly improved. The removal of these two main causes of Scottish discontent at home, almost completely stopped the migration to Ulster.

While the various attempts of the native Irish to regain the land always constituted some threat to the Scottish immigrants, this, too, came to an end. In 1690 William of Orange, a staunch Protestant, who had ascended the British throne a few years earlier, came to Ireland and defeated the deposed Catholic King James II at the Battle of the Boyne. The Scots thought that their troubles were now over. However, this was not to be the case.

While the immigrants to Ulster and their immediate descendants prospered in their new home, it was essentially this prosperity which led to the problems which eventually caused the 18th Century migration to America. The prosperity of Ulster came not only from the lush harvests of a fertile land, but also from two newly established industries, the weaving of woolen and linen fabrics. These industries started by the Scots flourished in the north of Ireland. This prosperous trade eventually ran counter to the fortunes of the English merchants and led to repressive measures against the Irish linen and woolen trades by the British Parliament. The final blow came, however, when the 31 year leases of some of the late 17th Century arrivals to Ulster expired. The long leases, at moderste rents, had encouraged the Scots to improve the land. At the expiration of the leases, the landlords either raised the rents exhorbitantly, or put the leases up for auction to the highest bidder. Many of the immigrants were forced to leave the land which they had improved.

Even this series of economic blows might not have been enough to cause the exodus which began in 1717, had not yet another thing happened. Frm 1714 to 1719 each year was noted for having insufficient rainfall. The continuous drought ruined the crops. With the loss of the flax crop, and the stricken flocks of sheep, the linen and woolen industries suffered. If these calamnities were not enough, there was added at this time, religious restrictions.

In the second year of the reign of Queen Anne (1703), the "Test Act" was passed requiring all office holders in Ireland to take the sacrament according to the rites of the Established Church of England (or Church of Ireland). The weight of this edict fell most heavily in Ulster upon the most influential members of the Presbyterian Church, who might be candidates for judgeships or other posts. This type of religious persecution was not unusual at that time. It was by no means uncommon for a sovereign to expect that his or her people would embrace their church. Scotland, at her Reformation had formed the Presbyterian Church as the "Kirk of Scotland". Although the Scots in Ulster had suffered some religious restrictions earlier, they had been able to make adjustments to these as their own church flourished. However, now in Queen Anne's day the Established Churdh Party was in power and they were determined to bring about conformity. They made use of the Test Act, which was aimed primarily at the Roman Catholics and turned against the Presbyterian Scots. It was used unscrupulously as a weapon to place the Presbyterians at the same level of disability as had been done with the Roman Catholics for many years. Ministers were turned out of their puplits, and the Scots were swept from such offices as constable, alderman or any civil post.

One of the effects of the Test Act was to silence the ministers who had talked against migration, when in 1716-17 such talk became more frequent. In fact, after the Test Act, no element of the Scottish population talked against moving, for all classes had been suppressed to some degree. The first migration from Ulster was then touched off by drought, depression and now by religious persecution. The exodus, when it came, was not a small trickle of discontented people. Among the first emigrants were ministers ready to lead their entire congregations to the New World. In 1717 more than 5000 Ulstermen left for America. Once favorable reports came back from the emigrants of 1717-18, it was easier for the others to follow. There were five great waves of emigration: 1717-18, 1725-29, 1740-41, 1754-55 and 1771-75.

While religious liberty was not the sole motivating factor in the beginning in 1717, it is significant to note that all of those who left Ulster were Presbyterians. Few Englishmen and fewer Irish Catholics left Ulster for America in this period. While many substantial citizens did leave Ulster, many of the poor did also. The one deterrent was the cost of the passage. This was overcome by many by selling themselves as "Indentured Servants" to pay their passage. Despite abuses in the indentured servant trade, it was this that permitted many of the lower classes to make the trip. Without this type of payment for passage, many might otherwise have had to stay behind in Ulster. Without this system, the colonies would have been denied the thing that they needed most--manpower.

CHAPTER II

THE SCOTCH-IRISH MIGRATION TO AMERICA

TIME AND PLACE OF SETTLEMENTS

There has been, from time to time, some confusion concerning the immigrant colonists from Scotland and the immigrant colonists from Ulster. By 1717 Scots and Ulstermen were two different nationalities. There was extensive immigration from Scotland itself in the 18th Century, but it amounted to only one-fourth or one-fifth as much as the immigration from Ulster. Prior to 1707 some Scots had come to the colonies as indentured servants to escape the poverty at home, while others were exiled as criminals. After 1707, when Union of the two Kingdoms of Scotland and England improved conditions in the Lowlands, there was no longer any large scale direct migration from the Lowlands of Scotland. However, there continued some occassional migration from the Highlands.

The Scots in America were clearly different from the Ulstermen. We will call the Ulstermen from this point on Scotch-Irish, although that term was not used until much later, as will be explained further on in this chapter. The Scots were seldom explorers and Indian fighters as were the Scotch-Irish.The Scots, for the main part, preferred to stay in the East and carry on business enterprises. At the time of the American Revolution, a more important difference can be noted between the two groups. The Scotch-Irish as a group were largely ardent patriots, while the Scots were, with some notable exceptions, Loyalists faithful to the Crown. Only in their Presbyterianism, and in a few other traits, did the Scots resemble the Scotch-Irish.

For the six decades following 1717, the Scotch-Irish immigrant tide flowed. America was strengthened by this new kind of settler, the typical pioneer who went beyond the outer fringes of civilization to establish himself on the frontier.

The size of the Scotch-Irish immigration is open to various estimates. There were no adequate statistics kept either in Ulster or in America for population or emigration. Historians generally agree that it was about 200,000, although some give higher estimates, some even as high as 300,000. The great variation in estimates is in part due to someone having found a factual figure for a particular year, and then assuming that it might have been the average, multiplied it by the number of years that the migration is known to have taken place. In some years the yearly figure did reach as high as 6,000. Scotch-Irish immigrant ships are known to have landed at most American ports, including Boston, Philadelphia, New York, Annapolis, Charleston and the Virginia ports. The best estimate for the number of persons of Scotch-Irish birth or ancestry in the United States in 1790, seems to be about 250-300,000. Again no exact figures are available. It is known though that the Scotch-Irish were the second largest nationality group in the United States at that time, with the English being first and the Germans third.

When the Scotch-Irish arrived in America they were not like the early English colonists arriving in Virginia, arriving in a country populated only by Indians. News from each colony was available in England and in Ulster. In making plans for the emigration, the leaders hardly considered the southern colonies since they were quite undeveloped. The already impoverished Ulsterman could see no hope in a slave owning region of large plantations. Maryland offered no great inducement since it, too, had a plantation economy, accompanied by a large number of Roman Catholics and a firmly established Church of England. New York was known to be hard on dissenters. Eliminating these, there was left only the middle colonies and New England. Reports from Penn's settlements were good. Those who had landed in Boston had unexpected difficulties and found a reception that lacked warmth. Those who entered America by the Delaware River, on the other hand, found a land of their hearts desire. The praise of the early settlers led others to follow. Throughout the six decades of the great Scotch-Irish migration, the greatest numbers arrived in America through Philadelphia and Chester, Pennsylvania and New Castle, Delaware. From there they headed west. The path that the immigrants followed to reach the frontier was determined by geography. The Great Valley of Pennsylvania led west for hundreds of miles. Then, blocked by the mountains, they turned south into the Shennandoah or Valley of Virginia. From there it was a short trip to the Piedmont region of the Carolinas. Thus as is shown in Figures 3 and 3A, there was a 700 mile arc, stretching from Philadelphia to the upper reaches of the Savannah River which became the new home of the Scotch-Irish.

The Scotch-Irish did not have the frontier to themselves. Arriving almost simultaneously with them were the German Palatines who were mostly Lutherans. Pennsylvania became the scene of alternating and parallel movements of the two people. The two groups generally stayed apart from each other, the Scotch-Irish settling in one part of a valley and the Germans in another. The next year's arrivals would then advance beyond the old settlements and thereby spread the process of civilizing the wilderness. Contact between the two groups in the first few years were generally minimal since they differed in language and custom. Most of the settlements were initially in the counties of Philadelphia, Chester, Berks and Lancaster.

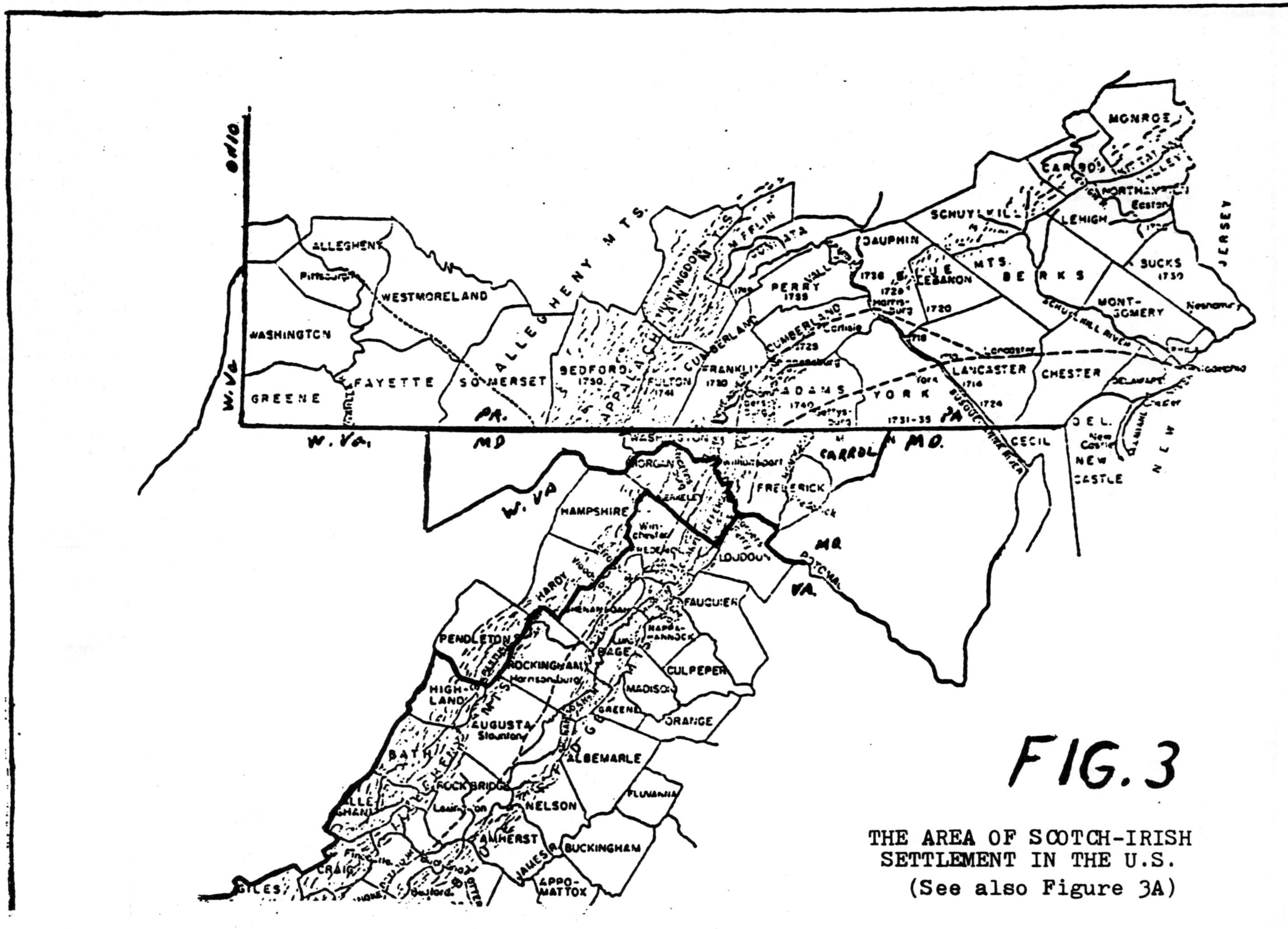

FIG. 3

THE AREA OF SCOTCH-IRISH SETTLEMENT IN THE U.S.
(See also Figure 3A)

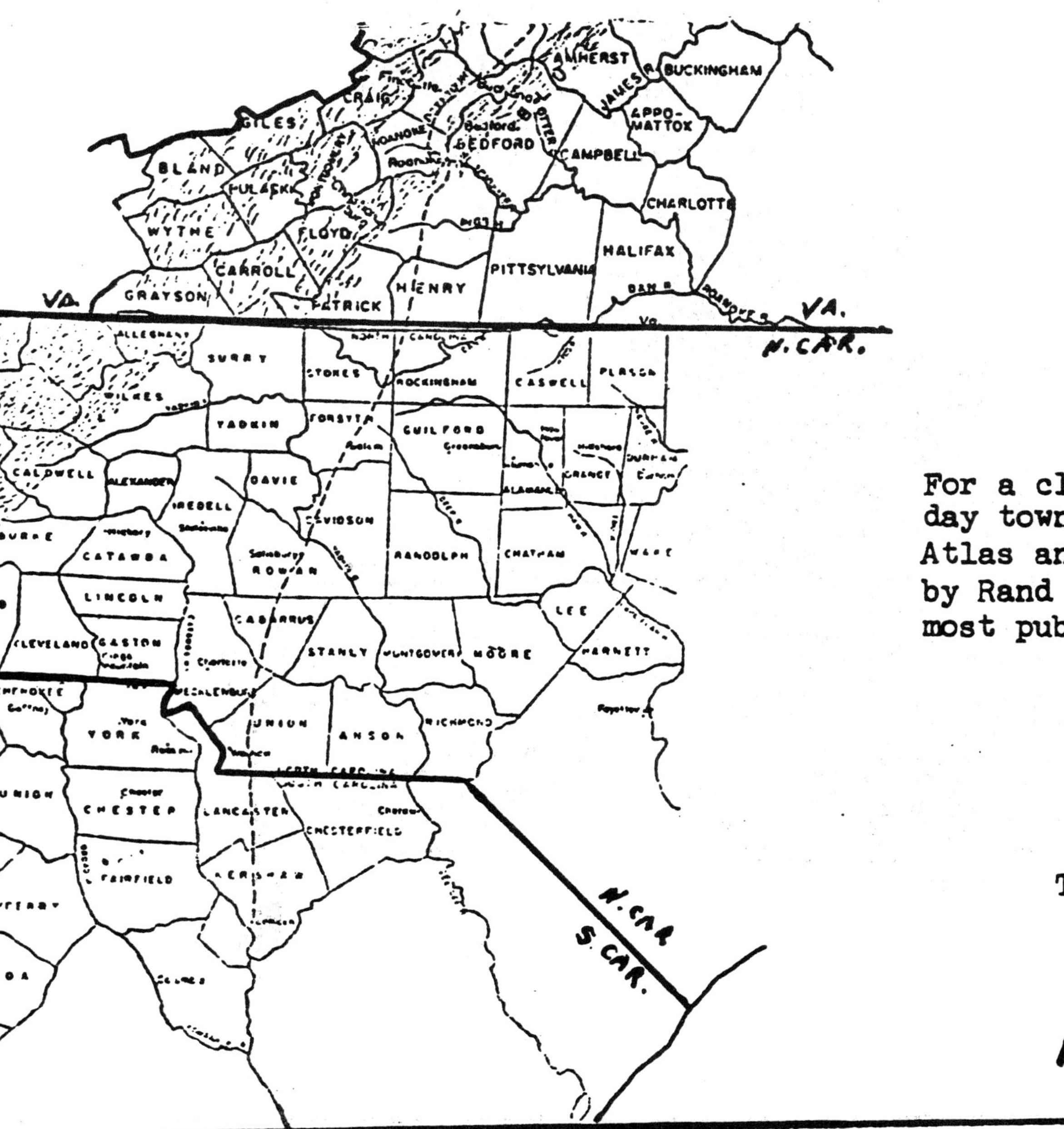

For a clear picture of present day towns, see "1974 Commercial Atlas and Marketing Guide" by Rand McNally, available in most public libraries.

THE AREA OF SCOTCH-IRISH SETTLEMENT IN THE U.S.

FIG. 3A

By 1730 they included York County and in 1740, Adams County. There were also settlements in Dauphin, Lebanon, Franklin, Fulton, Cumberland and Perry Counties with Bedford County being settled by 1750. The settlers generally avoided the disputed borderland between Pennsylvania and Maryland. After 1730 they began spilling southward, across Maryland into the valley of Virginia, into what are claimed now to be the most Scotch-Irish counties in the United States, Rockbridge, Augusta, etc. (See Figure 3).

While the tidewater area of Virginia had been settled earlier and was the scene of great plantations, the valley of the Shennandoah was almost empty. Some settlers had reached it as early as 1710 and there was one small Presbyterian community at Elizabeth River. By the 1740's the Scotch-Irish had gone as far south as the James River. When the settlements reached Roanoke, the valley ended. The settlers were now faced with the options of going westward across the mountains or turning eastward from Roanoke. Word spread quickly that land in the Carolinas was available, and the main stream of the migration then flowed toward the Carolina Piedmont. The Scotch-Irish and the Germans who had traversed the valley of Pennsylvania and the Shennandoah continued their travels. Few of them stopped to settle in the rugged hill country, instead their destination became the Piedmont region of North and South Carolina. While the early settlements in Pennsylvania and in Virginia had been contained to some extent by the mountains on either side of the valley, this was no longer the case in the Carolinas. The mountains were now far to the west, and the Piedmont lay before them in all directions.

In 1730 to 1750 a large number of Highland Scots had migrated directly from Scotland to North Carolina. These settlers coming by sea stayed generally near the coast, hardly any of them penetrated the Piedmont. Certainly some of the settlers of the Piedmont came from the Tidewater area, but the bulk of them came from Virginia and Pennsylvania. Some were new immigrants who, finding the valleys of Pennsylvania and Virginia densely populated, followed the inevitable course of the migration to the Carolinas. Others were already the second generation of Scotch-Irish who wanted to strike out on their own. While some of the transferees from Pennsylvania were Swiss, Welsh and Germans, by far the majority were Scotch-Irish, more than all of the other nationalities put together. Since there is no natural barrier between North and South Carolina, the land hungry settlers now crossed into the South Carolina Piedmont. It was about 1760 when the effective settlement of South Carolina by the Scotch-Irish began.

While this story has dwelt thus far mainly with the Scotch-Irish settlements in Pennsylvania, Virginia and the

Carolinas, it must be said that the Scotch-Irish settlements were not limited to these colonies. There is evidence that the Scotch-Irish settled in all of the thirteen original colonies.

It is estimated that as many as 20,000 Scotch-Irish may have settled in New England during the 18th Century. In 1718 between six and eight hundred arrived in Boston in five ships. They were mostly from the valley of the Bann in Coleraine (now Derry) in Ulster. They received a cool reception from the Puritans of Massachusetts. Their treatment was, however, no different than the treatment accorded to any outsiders. Some of the new immigrants moved on to Worcester which was then on the frontier. They formed a settlement which they named Coleraine. Others went as far west as Ostigo County, New York.

About one-fourth of the original group moved to Maine, settling around Wiscassett. Others went into what is now New Hampshire near Haverhill. One settlement was named Londonderry after the city in Ulster. There were two settlements in Vermont and one in Connecticutt near the present day town of Stirling. Boston was the only New England port which had significant Scotch-Irish immigration. However, some immigrants did arrive at Newport, Rhode Island in the 1740's.

The Middle Colonies, in general, attracted fewer Scotch-Irish immigrants than the rest of the colonies. Pennsylvania was the exception. As noted earlier, Philadelphia was one of the principal ports of entry during the Great Migration of the Scotch-Irish, although not all who entered through there stayed in Pennsylvania.

There were few settlements in New York. Most of these were Scotch-Irish who had originally come to Massachusetts and then moved west to Ostigo County. Other New York settlements were at Goshen, Walhill, Salem and Stillwater.

The port of New Castle, Delaware was, along with Philadelphia, a principal port of entry for the Scotch-Irish going to Pennsylvania. Only a few of them, however, stayed in Delaware. The colony of New Jersey became very important to many of the Scotch-Irish because the first college to educate Presbyterian ministers was established there in 1746. It was the Scots, rather than the Scotch-Irish, who were responsible for this institution. Few Scotch-Irish settled in New Jersey.

A considerable number of Scotch-Irish settled in Maryland. The western shore of Chesapeake Bay saw many indentured servants of Scotch-Irish background from Ulster. After their four year period of servitude was over, most of them moved on to Virginia or the Carolinas. The Scotch-Irish settlers on the eastern shore of Chesapeake Bay were among the first arrivals from Ulster and were among the first to intermingle with settlers of different origins and backgrounds.

While most of the Scotch-Irish who settled in the Carolinas arrived by way of Pennsylvania and Virginia, not all did. In the last two decades of the Great Migration a number of Scotch-Irish arrived directly in the Carolinas from from Belfast in Ulster. A number of immigrant ships arrived at Charleston in this period. A few of the immigrants settled in the Tidewater area but the majority moved on west to the Piedmont and beyond.

Georgia was the last of the colonies to be settled by the English. It was also not until the last decade before 1776 that the Scotch-Irish tide reached Georgia after rolling through the Carolina Piedmont. The colony had only a population of 2400 in 1752. By 1790, the time of the first census of the United States, there were 52,00 white inhabitants. Most of these were in the up country where the Scotch-Irish had settled, rather than in the plantations of the lower counties which had been the site of the first settlements in Georgia in 1733.

Toward the end of the Revolution, and shortly after it, many of the new Americans who prior to this time had settled in the areas east of the Appalachian Mountains, now turned their attention to the west. There is little doubt that the children of the Scotch-Irish immigrants were in the vanguard of the pioneers who settled in the areas to the west of the mountains. This generation of pioneers was, however, a generation of Americans, not of Englishmen, or Scotch-Irishmen, or Germans. Contrary to what has been written by some descendants of the Scotch-Irish, there was no great emphasis on their Scotch-Irish origin by the people who moved west. In fact, emphasis on national origin was not a characteristic of any of the people on the frontier. On the contrary, identification was most likely by their most recent place of origin, They were better known as Virginians, or North Carolinians. Under no circumstances would they call themselves Germans or Scotch-Irishmen.

Only near the end of the 19th Century, the late 1800's, did Americans, with a deepening consciousness of their history, start researching the distinctive contribution of any national group. This many times led to adulation of ancestors and sometimes exagerated claims for particular groups. For the greatest part of the century that intervened between the Scotch-Irish migration and the period after the Civil War, the very term "Scotch-Irish" did not appear.

The name "Scotch-Irish" contributed to quite a controversy. The American Irish Historical Society which was organized in 1897, devoted a great deal of time to deflating what they called "The Scotch-Irish Myth". They claimed that the people who came to the United States from from Ulster were Irish, not only geographically, but in patriotism for Ireland. It is a fact that the name Scotch-Irish is unknown in Ulster, that northern most province of Ireland from which the Scotch-Irish came. Although the Presbyterian Scots in Ulster did not have the long history of suffering at the hands of the English that the native and Anglo-Irish Catholics had, the Scots of Ulster had no great love for the English. By the time the migration to America came about, some of the Scots had been in Ireland for four or more generations and had become quite a different people from their forebears. No doubt by 1717 the Ulstermen looked upon themselves as Irish of the North. When they came to America, and when it was necessary to identify themselves officially, it was usuall as "Ulster-Irish", "Northern Irish" or "Presbyterian Irish". Most of the evidence shows that they accepted the designation as Irish naturally.

In 1737 the Ulstermen who had settled in Boston met with other Irishmen to celebrate St.Patrick's Day and organized themselves into a society known as "The Irish Society". During the Revolutionary War, an active group in Philadelphia was the Friendly Sons of St. Patrick, which consisted of Ulstermen and others from Ireland. The first president of the organization was the brother of a Catholic bishop and the second president was an Ulster Presbyterian.

The name Scotch-Irish seems to have first been used by Queen Elizabeth I in 1573, in reference to Highland Scots who had inter-married with the Irish. There are a number, possibly a dozen, references to the term Scotch-Irish that can be found in colonial writings. These seem insignificant, however, to the constantly appearing name of Irish.

In the century after the Revolution the name Scotch-Irish seems to have almost completely disappeared. It was the contention of the American Irish Historical Society that the name was revived after 1850 and enthusiastically used out of prejudice against the Irish of the south of Ireland who were then arriving in the United States in great numbers. While it is possibly true that prejudice played its part in popularizing the Scotch-Irish name, it is in fact a useful term. A century of use has now established the name and nothing else is really accurate. Originally "Irish Presbyterian" might have been used, but not after many of them became Baptists and Methodists on the frontier. Ulster Irish would not be right since it would not distinguish between the Scot, Englishman or native Irishman who lived in that northern province of Ireland. Ulster Scot would be more satisfactory except for the unfamiliarity of most Americans with the georaphic significance of Ulster. Since this would only be a reversal of the more usual "Scotch-Irish", it is best to retain that name, but to make its meaning clear.

CHAPTER III

BEGIN BY RESEARCHING YOUR

SCOTCH-IRISH ANCESTORS IN THE UNITED STATES

Before beginning to search for your ancestors in Northern Ireland or in Scotland, there is generally much work to be done concerning your American ancestors, that is, those descendants of your immigrant ancestor who originally came from Ireland. Since, as we stated earlier, the heaviest part of the Scotch-Irish immigration was from 1717 until the time of the American Revolution, there are usually numerous generations to be checked before reaching the immigrant ancestor.

Regardless of nationality, a family researcher should start with his immediate family. All research moves from the known to the unknown. Begin by talking to parents, grandparents, brothers, sisters, aunts and uncles. From them gather all of the facts that you can, no matter how seemingly unimportant some of the information may seem at the time. Of course, everything that you hear need not be accepted as absolute fact. It is all subject to further verification. You will no doubt get more than one version of the same event. It is not unusual, for example, for two older sisters to give different interpretations of some incident, or names of persons or places. Place names which older persons mention are often clues to the location in Northern Ireland or Scotland from which the family came. After you have gathered some information, do not delay in starting to put it into chart form, There are printed forms for this as illustrated in Figure 4, with instructions for completing the form in Figure 5.

It is just as well to start with a plain sheet of paper marked up in chart form, and then, after some clarification, transfer it to a neat printed form. Arrange this information starting with yourself as Number 1 on the chart. Arrange it in ascending order following the instructions in Figure 5. Do not attempt to put too much information on the chart, only the relevant dates and place names as shown. You will note that each person is given a number. This identifying number can then be used on another sheet to record everything that you have learned about each person on the chart. An example of a Family Group Record, for recording all information about a particular family group is shown on Figure 6. Plain paper with the identifying personal number or family group number can then be used for information not shown on either of the printed forms.

After you have completed the charts and recorded all of the information that you have accumulated, you will want to go

Ancestor Chart
Name of Compiler
Address
City, State
Date
Person No. 1 on this chart is the same person as No. ___ on chart No. ___.
Chart No.
b. Date of Birth
p.b. Place of Birth
m. Date of Marriage
d. Date of Death
p.d. Place of Death
1
b. p.b. m. d. p.d
2 (Father of No. 1)
b. p.b. m. d. p.d
3 (Mother of No. 1)
b. p.b. d. p.d.
4 (Father of No. 2)
b. p.b. m. d. p.d
5 (Mother of No. 2)
b. p.b. d. p.d.
6 (Father of No. 3)
b. p.b. m. d. p.d
7 (Mother of No. 3)
b. p.b. d. p.d.
8 (Father of No. 4)
b. p.b. m. d. p.d
9 (Mother of No. 4)
b. p.b. d. p.d
10 (Father of No. 5)
b. p.b. m. d. p.d
11 (Mother of No. 5)
b. p.b. d. p.d.
12 (Father of No. 6)
b. p.b. m. d. p.d
13 (Mother of No. 6)
b. p.b. d. p.d.
14 (Father of No. 7)
b. p.b. m. d. p.d
15 (Mother of No. 7)
b. p.b. d. p.d.
16 b. m. d. (Father of No. 8, Cont. on chart No.)
17 b. d. (Mother of No. 8, Cont. on chart No.)
18 b. m. d. (Father of No. 9, Cont. on chart No.)
19 b. d. (Mother of No. 9, Cont. on chart No.)
20 b. m. d. (Father of No. 10, Cont. on chart No.)
21 b. d. (Mother of No. 10, Cont. on chart No.)
22 b. m. d. (Father of No. 11, Cont. on chart No.)
23 b. d. (Mother of No. 11, Cont. on chart No.)
24 b. m. d. (Father of No. 12, Cont. on chart No.)
25 b. d. (Mother of No. 12, Cont. on chart No.)
26 b. m. d. (Father of No. 13, Cont. on chart No.)
27 b. d. (Mother of No. 13, Cont. on chart No.)
28 b. m. d. (Father of No. 14, Cont. on chart No.)
29 b. d. (Mother of No. 14, Cont. on chart No.)
30 b. m. d. (Father of No. 15, Cont. on chart No.)
31 b. d. (Mother of No. 15, Cont. on chart No.)
(Spouse of No. 1)
b. p.b. d. p.d.

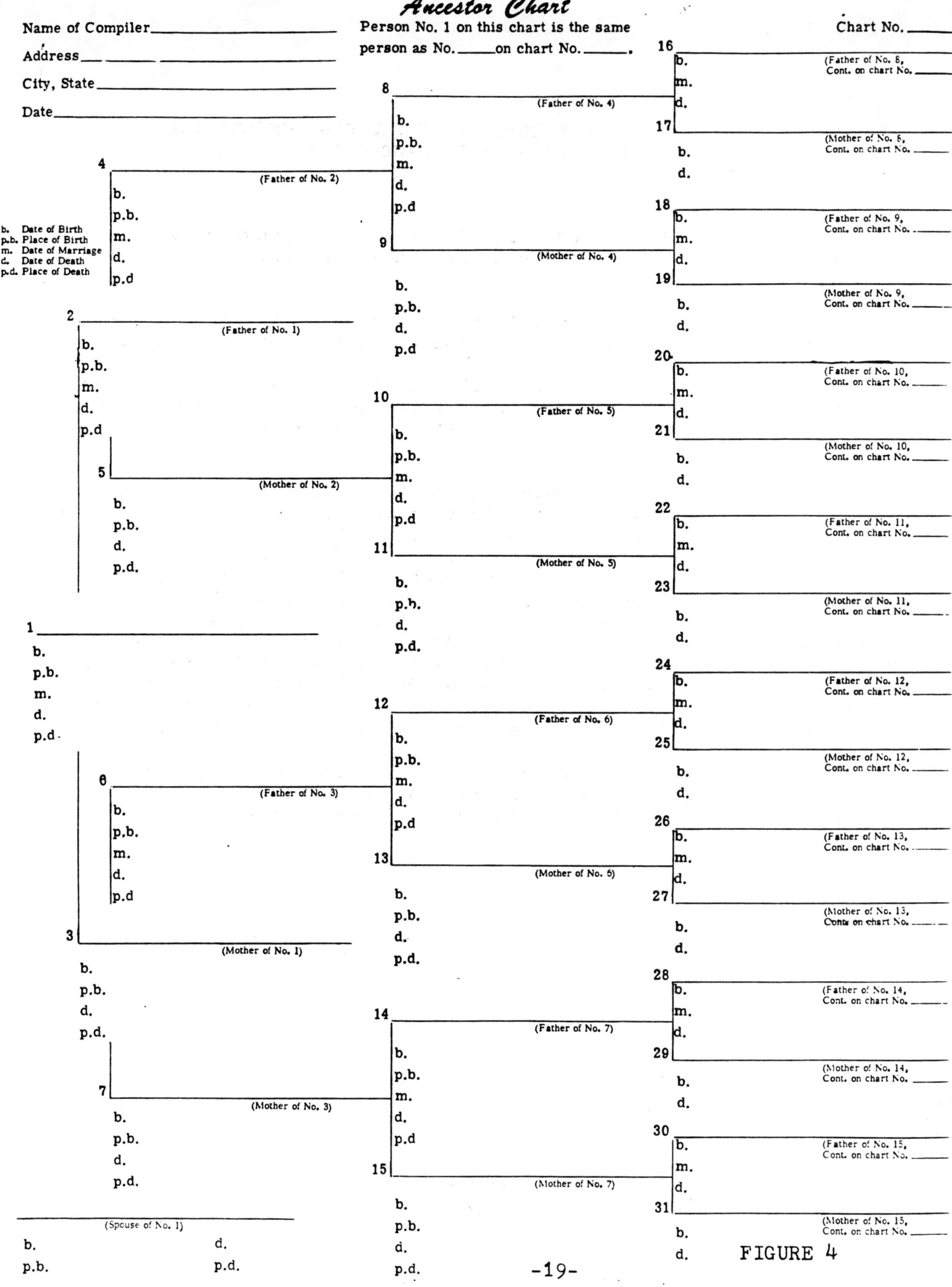

FIGURE 4

INSTRUCTIONS FOR COMPLETING THE FOUR GENERATION FIFTEEN NAME LINEAGE CHART

The chart may be extended indefinitely with progressive numbering, and new material may be put in its proper place without re-arranging data.

Place your name at Number 1 in the center of the first lineage chart. Mark this chart as No. 1 in the upper right hand corner.

Your father is No. 2, your mother is No. 3. Each father's number is double that of his son or daughter...2,4,6,8, etc. Each mother's number is double plus one....3,5,7, etc. Men's numbers are always even, womens numbers always uneven.

When you have reached No.8, if you have his father, you must go to another chart. Mark this new chart in the upper right hand corner "Chart 2 from Chart 1". Place the name of Number 8 in the left center of the chart in the space marked 1. You then "X" out the numeral 1 on this chart and write in his correct number "8". His father will then be Number 16, which you write in instead of the 2, which appears on the sheet. Number 8's mother will be Number 17. In the same manner, extend Number 9 from Chart 1 to the Number 1 spot on Chart 3 from Chart 1. Number 9's father becomes No. 18. Number 10 is extended on Chart 4, and so on. If Chart 2 ever needs to be extended, call the new chart, "Chart 2A", etc. Back on Chart No. 1, at the end of Number 8's line, fill in the blank space to read"Cont'd. on Chart No. 2".

You always have the same number for the same person, and as many charts as you extend, as many generations back as you trace, even though there may be omissions, there will always be a place for each person.

FIGURE 5

FAMILY RECORD

Surname ____________________
Family No. ____________________

FATHER Name in full ____________________

Event	Month Day Year	Town	County	State	Country
Birth					
Res.					
Married					
Death					
Burial					

His father's name ____________________ His mother's maiden name ____________________

MOTHER Name in full ____________________

Event	Month Day Year	Town	County	State	Country
Birth					
Res.					
Death					
Burial					

Her father's name ____________________ Her mother's maiden name ____________________

CHILDREN

Full given name	Event	Month Day Year	Town	County	State	Country	Cross Refer'nce Index
1	Birth						
Married to	Death						
	Mar.						
2	Birth						
Married to	Death						
	Mar.						
3	Birth						
Married to	Death						
	Mar.						
4	Birth						
Married to	Death						
	Mar.						
5	Birth						
Married to	Death						
	Mar.						
6	Birth						
Married to	Death						
	Mar.						
7	Birth						
Married to	Death						
	Mar.						
8	Birth						
Married to	Death						
	Mar.						
9	Birth						
Married to	Death						
	Mar.						
10	Birth						
Married to	Death						
	Mar.						
11	Birth						
Married to	Death						
	Mar.						
12	Birth						
Married to	Death						
	Mar.						

FIGURE 6

REVERSE SIDE for recording dates, locations and sources of information for each item:

back to some of the people to whom you have talked to double check data, and to gather more information if possible. It is amazing, how on a second visit, you are able to get additional information when you have the charts and other information to jog memories.

There will be gaps in the record, which will be apparent when looking at the chart. Some of the gaps can be filled in by writing to clergymen in the city or town in which your parents, grandparents, etc. have lived. While it can be done by writing, you can generally get better results if you can visit the town personally. Remember, in writing to clergymen, that it is common courtesy to include at least a self-addressed stamped envelope (referred to as SASE by genealogists). It might be well to also include a modest gratuity, because of the time spent researching the records and replying to your letter. At present with many people interested in genealogy, clergymen are receiving many inquiries about family records. To conscientiously reply to all of these requires a great deal of time. The author has found that many clergymen accept the gratuity gratefully while others return it with the reply.

As mentioned earlier, the Scotch-Irish were Presbyterians, almost without exception, when they migrated from Ulster. As they spread out on the American frontier, there sometimes were no Presbyterian ministers available, so they attended churches of other denominations. Particularly in Pennsylvania, some of them joined some of the predominantly German congregations of Unitarians, Lutherans and/or Baptists. The point is that while most were Presbyterians, in searching records do not overlook the possibility that they may have joined some other denomination. A good source to contact about Presbyterian Church Records is:

Presbyterian Historical Society
425 Lombard Street
Philadelphia, PA 19147

While you begin by tracing the families of your parents (two surnames), you will immediately become interested in other surnames as you reach the next generation (four surnames), and then eight surnames as you reach great-grandparents. Some of these may not be names of Scotch-Irish or Scot origin. Research them all, if you wish, until you reach the immigrant ancestor in each case. If you do, in fact, find ancestors who immigrated from places other than Ireland, they, too, can be researched, but the methods to be followed will not be touched upon in this book. You will find generally that your best information from relatives will concern the first two surnames, or possibly also those of your grandparents. The family relationship of people with the same surnames as some of your great-grandparents is now so distant that you may not know of anyone to whom you might write. This is particularly true if you are now living at a place some distance from the area where your great-grandparents lived. One point to remember in writing to any relatives, is to ask them for the names and addresses of people with the other surnames, to whom you might write. It is also well to realize that some of your relatives are not going to share your enthusiasm for researching the family history.

The best policy then is to write to all of the persons of the surnames in which you are interested and for whom you can get correct addresses. Quite often your letters will go unanswered, but don't let that discourage you. The occassional letter that does give additional information is well worth waiting for. When you cannot get the names and addresses of the more distant relatives from other family members, another source is to try the telephone books of the town or city in which your ancestor lived. Most public libraries have a wide selection of telephone books. Occassionally you may hit upon a person doing research on the same family name, in which case you might uncover a virtual treasure trove of information.

After you have exhausted the list of relatives, or even before that point, you may wish to try other sources. One source which has proven valuable to many family genealogists is the numerous compilations of a "Surname Index". Individuals or firms compile lists of persons researching particular surnames. For a small fee they will check their file and advise you of anyone that they know of, who is researching the same name that you are researching. They will add your name to their master index for reference to other people. You will find a number of these services advertised in each issue of THE GENEALOGICAL HELPER, a magazine to which every genealogist should be a subscriber. The address is: EVERTON PUBLISHERS, INC., P.O. Box 368, Logan, UT 84321. Write to them for current subscription information.

The GENEALOGICAL HELPER is also a wonderful source for the names of others who are researching the same surnames as you. Each year there are two exchange editions in which literally thousands of amateur genealogists place ads telling about the lines for which they are seeking information or have information to share. With the large number of people of Scotch-Irish descent in the United States, the correspondence method offers great possibilities. Again, anytime you correspond with an unknown correspondent, enclose an SASE. Another publication with a fine genealogical section and with queries is ANTIQUE WEEK/TRI-STATE TRADER. Although primarily a publication for antiquers, it covers a number of hobbies including genealogy. Write for information to AW/TST, Box 90, Knightstown, IN 46148. In addition to these two publications, there are genealogical query columns in more than 100 newspapers in the United States. A query placed in a newspaper in the area in which an ancestor lived can sometimes be very helpful. A good source to learn which newspapers have genealogical query columns is a book entitled: "Newspaper Genealogical Column Directory" by Anita Cheek Milner. It is available from Heritage Books, 1540 E. Pointer Ridge Place, Bowie, MD 20716. Write for current price.

Another source of information is the local historical or genealogical society in the area in which your ancestor lived. If you had several generations of ancestors in the same area, you might wish to join the society in that area. SUMMIT PUBLICATIONS publishes a book which lists the names and addresses of Genealogical Societies and Historical Societies throughout the United States.(See current Price List for cost.)

Because the Scotch-Irish migration was before the American Revolution many persons of Scotch-Irish ancestry have had family research done for the purpose of joining one of the many Hereditary and Patriotic Organizations, such as the Daughters of the American Revolution, Sons of the Revolution, Colonial Dames, etc.Membership in these societies requires documentation of the ancestry of prospective members. These documented registers offer another source of information for the person of Scotch-Irish ancestry. Most large public libraries have a copy of the DAR Patriot Index and some carry other society publications. Figure 7 lists the names and addresses of a number of these societies, which are concerned with the colonial and Revolutionary periods.

There were many county histories, published in the 1800's, which contain much genealogical information. Many have been recently reprinted and are advertised in the GENEALOGICAL HELPER and AW/TST (see above). There are a couple of ways to find which county histories are available. ANCESTRY, INC., Box 476, SALT LAKE CITY, UT 84110 has a book entitled "United States County History Catalog". It lists 3500 county history's housed in the Genealogical Society Library in Salt Lake City. The other source is a book entitled, "A Bibliography of American County Histories", by P.W. Filby. It is published by GENEALOGICAL PUBLISHING CO., 1001 N. Calvert St., Baltimore, MD 21202. One or both of these books are available in many libraries. Many of the county history's are available for rent or purchase. Another way of getting the information that you desire from a county history is to write to the Reference Librarian at the public library in the city which is the county seat of the county concerned. Such a request should include an SASE and at least 25 cents for each page you wish to have copied. Your local library will usually have a copy of the ALA Directory, that is, the AMERICAN LIBRARY ASSOCIATION DIRECTORY, which will give the name and address of every library in the United States. Ask the Reference Librarian to help you find this book.

When the research has taken you back to 1910 you will find that the federal census records are a valuable source of information. There are some important points to keep in mind in regard to the census records. The 1910 census records are the latest census records available for genealogical research at this time. It is

HEREDITARY AND PATRIOTIC ORGANIZATIONS FOR THE COLONIAL AND REVOLUTIONARY PERIODS

National Society, Daughters of the American Colonists (DAC)
2205 Massachusetts Ave., NW, Washington,DC 20008

Colonial Dames of America
421 E. 61st Street, New York, NY 10021

National Society of Colonial Dames of America
Dumbarton House, 2715 Q Street, Washington, DC 20007

National Society, Daughters of Colonial Wars
1307 New Hampshire Ave., Washington, DC 20009

National Society, Children of the American Colonists
2205 Massachusetts Ave., NW, Washington, DC 20008

National Society, Daughters of Founders and Patriots of America
1307 New Hampshire Ave., Washington, DC 20009

Order of the Founders and Patriots of America
c/o Federal Hall Memorial, 15 Pine St., New York, NY 10005

General Society, Sons of the Revolution
54 Pearl St., New York, NY 10004

National Society of the Children of the American Revolution
1776 "D" Street, NW, Washington, DC 20006

National Society, Sons of the American Revolution
1000 S. Fourth Street, Louisville, KY 40203

Hereditary Order of the Loyalists and Patriots of the American Revolution
2540 N. Randolph St., Arlington, VA 22207

National Society, Daughters of the American Revolution
1776 "D" Street, NW, Washington, DC 20006

FIGURE 7

expected that the 1920 records will become available in 1992. Census records for 1930 and later are not generally available for research. They are, however, available in certain cases as will be explained later. The census records that have been made available can be obtained are from the National Archives on microfilm. Many libraries have copies. They are available for reading at the National Archives in Washington and at the National Archives Field Branches. See Figure 8 for a list of locations. Census microfilm was, at one time, available on Inter-Libray Loan from the National Archives. This has been discontinued, but the service is now provided by a private firm on a fee basis. More about Inter-Libray Loan later. Ask your Reference Librarian if copies of census microfilm can be obtained. There are many persons and societies that have made printed copies of census records for their county. These printed copies are generally easier to use, since they are usually indexed and alphbetized. Many of these are available in large libraries. Many researchers who have access to a large number of census records at their local library, will provide a census search service for a fee. Such people advertise their services in genealogical periodicals such as the GENEALOGICAL HELPER.

Since there will be more than one generation of your family in the United States before 1920, the census records will help you trace from one generation to another back to 1790. The early census records provided only a small amount of information about each household, with only the head of the household being listed individually. Starting with 1850 each individual was listed. Each succeeding census carries additional information. The 1880,1900 and 1910 census records provide a lot of information about each individual. See Figures 9 and 9A for details of the kind of information that is found in the census record for each particular year. Of particular importance are the later records which indicate place of birth and place of father and mother's birth.

As you begin checking census records, and particularly if you are reading ads offering census search service, you will hear about the SOUNDEX INDEX SYSTEM. This is usually just referred to as the 1880 Soundex or the 1900 Soundex. The Soundex is a system by which these particular years census entries were coded and indexed. For the 1880 census, only the households in which there was a child 10 years of age, or younger, were indexed. This limits the use of this index if you are searching for elderly people. The 1900 census, however, was completely indexed by the Soundex system. The main value of the Soundex, then, is that for the 1900 census, and for 1880, you may be able to locate a person fairly easily even if you don't know the name of the county or town. You must know the state or be prepared to search several possible states.

In order to use the Soundex, you must learn to translate the surnames that you are searching into the Soundex Code so that you can locate the proper census roll to read. The filing system is by state, then by first letter of the surname and numeric thereafter.

NATIONAL ARCHIVES FIELD BRANCHES

For each of the following, address inquiries to:

Director, National Archives (name of city) Branch

BOSTON
380 Trapelo Rd.
Waltham, MA 02154
(617) 647-8100

NEW YORK
Bldg. 22 MOT Bayonne
Bayonne, NJ 07002
(201) 823-7252

PHILADELPHIA
9th and Market Sts.
Philadelphia, PA 19107
(215) 597-3000

ATLANTA
1557 St. Joseph Ave.
East Point, GA 30344
(404) 763-7477

CHICAGO
7358 South Pulaski Rd.
Chicago, IL 60629
(312) 581-7816

KANSAS CITY
2312 East Bannister Rd.
Kansas City, MO 64131
(816) 926-7271

DENVER
Bldg. 48, Denver Fed. Ctr.
Denver, CO 80225
(303) 236-0818

SAN FRANCISCO
1000 Commodore Drive
San Bruno, CA 94066
(415) 876-9009

LOS ANGELES
24000 Avilla Road
Laguna Niguel, CA 92677
(714) 643-4220

SEATTLE
6125 Sand Point Way NE
Seattle, WA 98115
(206) 526-6507

FORT WORTH
501 West Felix St.
(P.O. Box 6216)
Ft. Worth, TX 76115
(817) 334-5525

FIGURE 8

CENSUS DATA - (1790-1860)

CENSUS OF 1790 - Name of head of family; address; number of free white males age 16 and up, including heads of family; free white males under age of 16; free white females, including heads of family; all other free person; number of slaves.

CENSUS OF 1800 - Name of head of family; address; number of free white males and females under age 10, 10 and under 16, 16 and under 26, 26 and under 45, 45 and up; all other free persons except Indians not taxed; number of slaves.

CENSUS OF 1810 - Same as 1800.

CENSUS OF 1820 - Name of head of family; address; number of free white males and females under age 10, 10 and under 16, 16 and under 26, 26 and under 45, 45 and up; number of free white males between 16 and 18; foreigners not naturalized; male and female slaves and free colored persons under 14, 14 and under 26, 26 and under 45, 45 and up; all other free persons except Indians not taxed; number of persons (including slaves) engaged in agriculture, commerce and manufacture.

CENSUS OF 1830 - Name of head of family; address; number of free white males and females in 5 year age groups to 20, 10 year age groups 20 to 100 and older; number of slaves and free colored persons in 6 broad age groups; number of deaf and dumb in 3 age groups; number of blind; foreigners not naturalized.

CENSUS OF 1840 - Name of head of family; address; number of free white males and females in age groups as in 1830; number of slaves and free colored persons in 6 age groups; number of deaf and dumb; number of blind; number of insane and idiotic in public and private charge; number of persons in each family in 7 occupational groups; number of schools and number of scholars; number of white persons over 20 who can read and write; number of pensioners for Revolutionary or military service.

CENSUS OF 1850 - Name; address; age; sex; color (white black or mulatoo) for each person; whether deaf, dumb, blind, insane or idiotic; all free persons required to give value of real estate owned; profession, occupation or trade for each male over 15; place of birth; whether married within year; whether attended school within year; whether unable to read and write for persons over 20; whether pauper or convict.

CENSUS OF 1860 - Essentially the same as 1850.

FIGURE 9

CENSUS DATA (1870-1910)

CENSUS of 1870 - Address; name; age; sex; color (including Chinese and Indian); citizenship, males over 21; profession, occupation or trade; value real estate; value personal estate; place of birth, whether father or mother were foreign born; born within year; married within year; attended school within year; for persons age 10 and over whether able to read and write; whether deaf, dumb, blind, insane or idiotic.

CENSUS of 1880 - Address; name; relationship to head of family; sex; race; age; marital status; born within year; married within year; profession, occupation or trade; number of months unemployed during census year; whether person is sick or temporarily disabled so as to be unable to attend to ordinary business or duties, if so, what is the sickness or disability; whether blind, deaf, dumb, idiotic, insane, maimed, crippled or bed-ridden; attended school within the year; ability to read and write; place of birthof father and mother.

CENSUS of 1890 - Address; number of families in house;number of persons in house; number of persons in family; name; whether soldier, sailor or marine during Civil War(Union or Confederate) oe widow of such a person; relationship to head of family; white, black, mulatoo, quadroon, octoroon, Chinese, Japanese or Indian; sex; age; marital status; whether married during the year; mother-how many children, and how many now living; place of birth of person, father, mother; if foreign born, how many years in the U.S.; whether naturalized; whether papers taken out; profession,etc.; months employed during the year; ability to read and write; speak English, if not, what language spoken; suffering from disease, with name of disease and length of time afflicted; whether defective in mind, sight, hearing or speech or whether crippled, maimed or deformed, with name of defect; whether a prisoner, convict, homeless child or pauper; home rented or owned by head or family member, is it free from mortgage; if head of family is farmer, is farm rented or owned by him or family member; if owned, is it free of mortgage, if mortgaged give post office address of owner.

CENSUS of 1900 - Name; address; relationship od each person to the head of family; color or race; sex; date of birth, age at last birthday; marital status, number of years married; mother of how many children, number of these children living; place of birth; place of birth of father and mother; year of immigration to U.S., if immigrant; and number of years in U.S.; whether naturalized; profession, etc. of each person over 10 years of age; number of months unemployed during the year; number of months attended school during the year; ability to read or write; ability to speak English; whether owns or rents; whether owns free of mortgage; whether a farm or a house.

CENSUS of 1910 - Essentially the same as 1900.

FIGURE 9A

It keeps together names of the same and similar sound, but of variant spelling.

The following guide will show you how to code a surname so that you can search for it in the Soundex.

SOUNDEX CODING GUIDE

Code	Key Letters and Equivalents
1	b, p, f, v
2	c, s, k, g, j, q, x, z
3	d, t
4	l
5	m, n
6	r

No code number is given to the letters a, e, i, o, u, y, w and h.

No number is assigned to the first letter of the surname.If the name is Brown the index card will be in the "B" segment of the index. The Code Number for Brown is 650 or rather B 650. Every Soundex Code must be a three digit number. A zero is added if necessary to any numbers to make it three digits. For example the name BROWN: B is not coded; r = 6; o is not coded; and n = 5. This gives you B 65. As this is only two digits, a zero is added to make it three digits. Hence, BROWN is B 650. No more than three digits are ever used in this system. Even if there are more letters, you stop after threedigits. Hence, BROWN is coded as B- 650. No more than three digits are ever used in this system. Even if there are additional letters, you stop after three digits.Also it is important to know that when a double letter occurs it is coded as a single letter - by a single digit. An example would be COLLINS, which is C-452. C is not coded; o is not coded; ll is coded as one letter by the numeral 4; i is not coded; n = 5; and s = 2. Therefore COLLINS is coded C- 452.

After locating a name in the Soundex, you may wish to have the full census information. The Soundex card will refer you to the proper county, town and page to check.

If you obtain your information from one of the printed census schedules and later wish to have a copy of the original census listing for your family history book, they are available from the National Archives. They will not make a search for you, but if you can provide the page number, they do provide the photocopy service.

Now let's go back to the census records of 1930 and later, which we said are not generally available for genealogical research. Information taken in 1920 and later is available from the Personal Census Service Branch, Bureau of the Census, Pittsburg, KS 66762, subject to the following restrictions:

For an adult -- must be requested by the individual concerned.

For a minor child -- must be requested by a parent or guardian.

For a deceased person -- must be requested by a blood relative of the immediate family (parent, brother, sister or child), surviving husband or wife, beneficiary with legal evidence of this relationship, or the executor of an estate with a court order of the appointment. Requests must be accompanied by a certified copy of the Death Certificate of the deceased, and the relationship of the requestor to the deceased must be indicated.

A remittance must accompany all requests for searches. Write for current fee schedule. Searches are conducted in the order of arrival of the requests. The fee covers the search of not more than two censuses for one applicant, and the results are furnished for one fee. If additional copies are wanted, there is an additional fee. Full schedules (for genealogical purposes) will be furnished for a fee. The full schedule is the complete one line of information recorded for the individual. The name of the head of the household will be given but the names of other individuals in the household will not be listed.

The Bureau of the Census does not issue Birth Certificates. However, it does furnish a transcript of census records, which in many cases will be accepted in place of a Birth Certificate, if such a certificate cannot be located elsewhere.

Write to the Bureau of the Census at the address given above for a form on which to apply for a census search, and for further details on fees charged.

The local public library will usually be the first library in which the genealogical researcher will attempt to do research. If the library happens to be large enough to have a Local History and Genealogy Section, it will no doubt have a sizeable amount of material on colonial and Scotch-Irish settlement. If it is a small library without a Local History and Genealogy Section, it may still provide very valuable help to you through Inter-library Loan. Inter-Library Loan was mentioned earlier in connection with microfilm copies of the census lists. For those not familiar with Inter-Library Loan, a few words of explanation may be necessary. If your local library does not have a particular book which you would like to see, they may obtain it for you from the state library or other library which may have the book. If you do not know where a particular book may be found, the librarian can determinine this by referring to the The National Union Catalog. The NUC is published by the Library of Congress.Most large libraries have a set of these books or can check them by phone at a nearby larger library. You might also check with the Library of Congress by mail. The NUC lists books held by all of the major libraries in the United States. Consult the Reference Librarian in your local library about Inter-Library Loan. Once the availability of the book is known, your library will request the book on loan. When the book arrives, you will be notified and you may check it out in the normal manner, unless the lending library has placed a restriction that it must be used in the library. This often happens with old and unusual books. You may be asked to pay a small charge to cover the cost of mailing the book. Many libraries also make microfilm available through Inter-library Loan. Until 1981 the National Archives loaned microfilm through the libraries. This service was abolished because of budget cuts. A private firm now loans National Archives microfilm through the libraries for a fee. Ask your Reference Librarian about this service. Most libraries participate. The costs are modest.

Lists of the various types of microfilm available from the National Archives can be obtained by writing to:

National Archives
National Archives and Record Service
Washington,DC 20408

It was earlier suggested that you start with church records rather than civil records. The reason for this is that there might be more continuity to the record trail with the church records since they have existed for a much longer time. Civil records, or at least the central repositories for vital statistics, did not begin in most states until the early 20th Century. The list of dates for each state is shown in Figure 10.These records may help you get back to the point where the census records are of help. To determine to whom you shoud write in each state for civil records, first obtain information from:

Superintendent of Documents
U.S. Government Printing Office
Washington,DC 20402

Write to that address for ordering information for three booklets which they produce. The cost is modest. The three booklets are:

"Where to Write for Birth and Death Records"DHEW Pub. (PHS)78-1142
"Where to Write for Marriage Records"DHEW Pub. (PHS)78-1144
"Where to Write for Divorce Records"DHEW Pub. (PHS)78-1145

Another source of information for the genealogist is the court record of wills. Older wills quite often provide some genealogical information and occassioally a place of birth. Not all of your ancestors will have executed a will, but some probably did, so this area should not be overlooked as a source of information. In most states it is necessary to write to the Clerk of the Probate or County Court for a copy of an ancestor's will. Write and request the fee for a search and a copy of the will if it exists. The correct place to write for each state is shown in Figure 11. Figure 12 gives a list of court terms and their definitions which would be useful in understanding the will if you do get a copy.

Another type of federal record of help to the genealogist is

BIRTH AND DEATH REGISTRATION

State	Required By Law	90% Completeness	
		Birth	Death
Alabama	1908	1927	1925
Alaska	1960(1913)	1950	1950
Arizona	1909	1926	1926
Arkansas	1914	1927	1927
California	1905	1919	1906
Colorado	1907	1928	1906
Connecticutt	1897	1915	1890
Delaware	1881	1921	1890
Dist. of Columbia	b.1873,d.1854	1915	1880
Florida	1899	1924	1919
Georgia	1919	1928	1922
Hawaii	b.1847,d.1841	1929	1917
Idaho	1911	1926	1922
Illinois	1916	1922	1918
Indiana	1907	1917	1900
Iowa	1880	1924	1923
Kansas	1911	1917	1914
Kentucky	1911	1917	1911
Louisiana	1918	1927	1918
Maine	1892	1915	1900
Maryland	1898	1916	1906
Massachusetts	1841	1915	1880
Michigan	b.1906.d.1898	1915	1900
Minnesota	1908	1915	1910
Mississippi	1912	1921	1919
Missouri	1910	1927	1911
Montana	1907	1922	1910
Nebraska	1904	1920	1920
Nevada	1911	1929	1929
New Hampshire	1883	1915	1890
New Jersey	1878	1921	1880
New Mexico	1920	1929	1929
New York(exc.NYC)	1915	1915	1890
North Carolina	1913	1917	1910
North Dakota	1907	1924	1924
Ohio	1908	1917	1909
Oklahoma	1917	1928	1928
Oregon	1903	1919	1918
Pennsylvania	1906	1915	1906
Rhode Island	1896	1915	1890
South Carolina	1915	1919	1916
South Dakota	1920	1932	1906
Tennessee	1914	1927	1917
Texas	1903	1933	1933
Utah	1905	1917	1910
Vermont	1919(1777)	1915	1890
Virginia	1912	1917	1913
Washington	1907	1917	1908
West Virginia	1925	1925	1925
Wisconsin	1907	1917	1908
Wyoming	1909	1922	1922

FIGURE 10

CUSTODIANS OF WILLS AND ADMINISTRATIONS

ALABAMA-------------Clerk, Probate Court, County Seat
ARIZONA-------------Clerk of Superior Court, County Seat
ARKANSAS------------Clerk, Probate Court, County Seat
CALIFORNIA----------County Clerk, County Seat
COLORADO------------County Clerk, County Seat
CONNECTICUTT--------State Librarian, Hartford, CT
DELAWARE------------Public Archives Commission, Dover, DE
DIST. OF COLUMBIA---Register of Wills, Court House
FLORIDA-------------Clerk, County Court, County Seat
GEORGIA-------------Clerk, Court of Ordinary, County Seat
HAWAII--------------Clerk, Circuit Court
IDAHO---------------Clerk, Probate Court, County Seat
ILLINOIS------------Clerk, Probate Court, County Seat
INDIANA-------------Clerk, Circuit Court, County Seat
IOWA----------------County Clerk, County Seat
KANSAS--------------Clerk, Probate Court, County Seat
KENTUCKY------------Clerk, County Court, County Seat
LOUISIANA-----------Clerk in District Court in parish
MAINE---------------Register of Probate, County Seat
MARYLAND------------The Hall of Records, Annapolis,MD
MASSACHUSETTS-------Register of Probate, County Seat
MICHIGAN------------Clerk, Probate Court, County Seat
MINNESOTA-----------Clerk, Probate Court County Seat
MISSISSIPPI---------Clerk, Court of Chancery, County Seat
MISSOURI------------Clerk, Probate Court, County Seat
MONTANA-------------Clerk, District Court, County Seat
NEBRASKA------------Clerk, County Court, County Seat
NEVADA--------------County Clerk, County Seat
NEW HAMPSHIRE-------Register of Probate, County Seat
NEW JERSEY----------Clerk, Orphan's & Surrogate Ct., Co. Seat
NEW MEXICO----------Clerk, Probate Court, County Seat
NEW YORK------------Clerk, Surrogate Court, County Seat
NORTH CAROLINA------Clerk, Superior Court, County Seat
NORTH DAKOTA--------Clerk, County Court, County Seat
OHIO----------------Clerk, Probate Court, County Seat
OKLAHOMA------------Clerk, County Court, County Seat
OREGON--------------County Clerk, County Seat
PENNSYLVANIA--------Register of Wills, County Seat
RHODE ISLAND--------Clerk, Probate Ct.Civil Div., County Seat
SOUTH CAROLINA------Clerk, Probate Court, County Seat
SOUTH DAKOTA--------County Clerk County Seat
TENNESSEE-----------County Clerk, County Seat
TEXAS---------------County Clerk, County Seat
UTAH----------------County Clerk, County Seat
VERMONT-------------Probate Court. County Seat
VIRGINIA------------Clerk, Circuit Court, County Seat
WASHINGTON----------County Clerk, County Seat
WEST VIRGINIA-------County Clerk, County Seat
WISCONSIN-----------County Clerk, County Seat
WYOMING-------------County Clerk, County Seat

FIGURE 11

SOME COURT TERMS AND THEIR DEFINITIONS

ADMINISTRATOR-------	The one legally authorized to settle or manage an estate.
ADMINISTRATRIX------	Female administrator.
ALIEN---------------	To transfer property.
APPRAISER-----------	Specifically one vested with authority to determine the value of property.
CODICIL-------------	An instrument made subsequently to a will and modifies it in some respect. Can add provisions and update.
COEXECUTOR----------	A joint executor.
CURATOR-------------	(1) A person appointed temporarily, such as a sheriff or other public officer, until the administrator of the estate is named. (2) A guardian appointed for minors or others past the age of pupillarity (generally fourteen years for males and twelve for females.)
DEVISE--------------	To give by will, especially real estate.
DEVISEE-------------	Person who receives land or other property by will.
DEVISOR-------------	Testator, one who wills to another.
DOWER--------------- (dower right)	That portion of, or interest in, the real estate of a deceased husband which the law gives for life to the widow.
EXECUTOR------------ (Executrix)	Person (or persons) appointed or named in will to administer the testator's will.
ENDOW---------------	To furnish with money or its equivalent as a permanent fund for support.
ET ALL--------------	And others.
ET UXOR------------- (et ux)	And wife.
FEE-----------------	An estate of inheritance in land.
FEE SIMPLE----------	A fee without limitation to any class of heirs or restriction on alienation.
FEE TAIL------------	An estate of inheritance limited to a class of heirs.
HEIR----------------	Any person inheriting any property of a deceased person.
IMPRIMIS------------	In the first place.
IMPUTE--------------	To impose as a charge.
INTESTATE-----------	Without having made a valid will.
INVENTORY-----------	A catalogue or account of the whole of an estate and its worth.
LEGATEE-------------	One to whom a legacy is bequeathed.
NOLLE PROSEQUI------	An entry on the record denoting that the prosecutor or plantiff will proceed no further in his action or suit, either as a whole, or as to some count.
NON PROSEQUITOR----- (non pros)	A judgement against the plaintiff in a suit where he does not appear to prosecute.
NUNCUPATIVE---------	Oral; not written.
PROBATE-------------	Act or process proving the last will.
OBIT SINE-----------	Dead without issue.
TESTATE ESTATE------	Estate which is disposed of by will.
TESTATOR------------	Person who died leaving a will.
TRUSTEE-------------	Person to whom property is vested in trust for others.

FIGURE 12

the Naturalization Records. These generally are not of much help as far as the Scotch-Irish ancestor is concerned since the Scotch-Irish who arrived during the Great Migration automatically became citizens upon the formation of the United States. The Naturalization Records may, however, be of some value in tracing collateral lines during the 19th Century. Among the information contained in the Naturalization Record is the date and place of arrival of a person into the United States. Also the date and place from which the person emigrated. They usually provide a clue as to the name of the ship on which the person arrived, which may be helpful in locating the actual Passenger List of that ship. More about Passenger Lists later.

The search for Naturalization Records is divided into two parts. First, those who were naturalized prior to September 27, 1906; and secondly, those naturalized after that date. In the case of those naturalized after 1906, the Immigration and Naturalization Service in Washington, DC has duplicate copies of all naturalization records. A master index of all the files created since September 27, 1906 has been established. A request for a search of the record of an ancestor naturalized after September 27, 1906 can be made on Form N-585 which can be obtained from any office of the Immigration Service. Consult the phone book of any large city or write to:

Immigration and Naturalization Service
Washington, DC 20536

This form must be accompanied by the fee indicated on the form. An employee of the Naturalization Service will search the files and supply the requested information. In addition, they will supply the name of the court which granted naturalization. If the Naturalization Service does not supply all of the information desired and which can be expected from a Naturalization Certificate, the next step would be to contact the court.

Prior to 1906, Naturalization Certificates were issued by local courts. The law did not specify particular courts to engage in naturalization, so there were a variety of courts which granted certificates -- federal courts, state courts, county courts and local courts. Any court having common law jurisdiction could naturalize foreigners provided that they met the federal requirements. The courts generally retained the documents filed by the applicant. Some transferred records to a state depository and occassionally to a federal court. In some cases only copies were transferred.

Until December 5, 1972 it was unlawful to copy immigration papers. The law was changed and it is now legal for a court to copy immigration records without notifying the Immigration and Naturalization Service. In 1973 the Immigration and Naturalization Service notified the 1000 or more courts now engaged in naturalization of the change in the law. It may be many more years before all Clerks of Courts, not now engaged in naturalization are made aware of the change in the law. It may be n ecessary for a researcher to call this new policy to the attention of the clerks and invite them to contact the nearest immigration office for a review of the current procedure. Some researchers have found this to be necessary when a clerk, who had not heard of the change, refused to allow them to copy the records of their immigrant ancestors.

A researcher may have to contact more than one court in the area in which the immigrant ancestor lived until they find the right one, if the ancestor was naturalized before 1906. In this case you may wish to consult the following book before proceeding:

"Locating Your Immigrant Ancestor-
A Guide to Naturalization Records"
by James C. and Lila Lee Neagles --1975
Pub. by: The Everton Publishers, Inc.
P.O. Box 368
Logan,UT 84321

This book gives a state by state, county by county, list of records available. It also lists federal courts in each state which have records.

Modern ship's passenger lists are not of value in finding information about Scotch-Irish ancestors who arrived prior to 1790. Of course, some researchers will have ancestors who arrived after that date, so some discussion of passenger lists in the National Archives could be helpful. Some older passenger lists exist and these will be mentioned later.

There are two kinds of federal passenger lists since 1790. The one kind, Customs Passenger Lists, were made primarily for taxation purposesand the people shown on them would be primarily visitors, rather than immigrants; hence, they seldom provide much information for the genealogical researcher. The Immigrant Passenger Lists, on the other hand, contain the names of persons coming to the United States with the fixed intention of becoming permanent settlers. Immigration Passenger Lists of the early years are quite sketchy. The do, however, include the individuals name and country of origin, as well as age, sex and occupation. On some of the newer records, occassionally the name of a relative in the United States is given. This is very rare, however. The locality information is usually very general, giving only the country name.

Locating an immigrant's name on a passenger list can present quite a problem. Many of them are not indexed. If your ancestor arrived during the years that are indexed the problem is not too great, if you know approximately the right year, even if you don't know the name of the ship. It will take some time but not nearly as much as for the years that are not indexed. You can cut down the amount of time by only checking lists for ships leaving particular ports from which an ancestor may have emigrated.

Records of Immigration Passenger Lists that are less than fifty years old are not available for research. All of the records are stored in the National Archives in Washington, DC, but are also at some of the Branch Offices for viewing on microfilm. More information about the availability of Immigration Passenger Lists, including years indexed, can be found in a book published by the National Archives. It is entitled:"A Guide to Genealogical Records in the National Archives". It may be purchased from:

The National Archives
National Archives and Record Service
Washington,DC 20408

Write for price and ordering information. The addresses of the National Archives Branch Offices are given in Figure 8. It is best to call or write first to determine if a particular center has the lists in which you are interested.

There have been a number of books published in the last several years which will help to locate immigrant on ship's passenger lists, even lists from ships arriving before 1790. Among these books are:

"Passenger and Immigration Lists Index" (3 volumes). Edited by P.William Filby and Mary K. Meyer. Published by Gale Research Co., Book Tower, Detroit,MI 48226.

"Bibliography of Ship's Passenger Lists (1538-1900". Edited by P. William Filby. Pub. by Gale Research Co., Detroit,MI 48226

"Ships Passenger Lists:National and New England"by Carl Boyer, 3rd.
"Ships Passenger Lists:New York and New Jersey"by Carl Boyer,3rd.
"Ships Passenger Lists:The South", by Carl Boyer,3rd.
"Ships Passenger Lists:Pennsylvania and Delaware" by Carl Boyer,3rd.
These are all for sale through The Augustan Society, P.O. Box P, Torrance, CA 90501
"Passengers to America" edited by Michael Tepper. Pub. by Genealogical Publishing Co., 1001 N. Calvert St., Baltimore, MD 21202.

There is no one all inclusive source for checking passenger lists of the Scotch-Irish. Many such lists, however, have been abstracted from newspapers and periodicals of the time. Quite a number were published in the JOURNAL OF THE AMERICAN-IRISH HISTORICAL SOCIETY. Copies of these journals are available in many large public and historical society libraries. It can be expected that if the current interest in genealogy continues, there will be additional information published in regard to Passenger Lists as well as on other genealogical subjects.

The New England Historic Genealogical Society at 101 Newberry St., Boston, MA 02116 has lending library privileges for its members. It has one of the finest collections of books on colonial ancestry, including the Scotch-Irish. Joining this society could really benefit anyone researching colonial ancestry.

There is a periodical aimed specifically at those researching colonial ancestry. This could also be of help in researching Scotch-Irish ancestry. Help may be obtained either from its content or from contacts made through its query columns. The periodical is THE COLONIAL GENEALOGIST, published by the AUGUSTAN SOCIETY, P.O. Box P, Torrance, CA 90501. Write for subscription information.

There is a new Scotch-Irish Newsletter available. It is published 3 times per year. This may provide some valuable contacts for research. It is published by: Jeff Williamson, 4631 -- 141st Street W., Apple Valley, MN 55124. Write for price and more details.

The catalogs of the following all contain books and pamphlets of interest to Scotch-Irish and other researchers:THE BOOKMARK, P.O. Box 74, Knightstown, IN 46148; GENEALOGICAL PUBLISHING CO., 1001 N. Calvert St., Baltimore, MD 21202; GENEALOGY UNLIMITED,Inc., P.O. Box 537, Orem, UT 84059; HERITAGE BOOKS, 1540 E Pointer Ridge Place, Bowie, MD 20716; YE OLDE GENEALOGIE SHOPPE, P.O. Box 39128, Indianapolis, IN 46239

There are some very rare and/or out of print books which cannot be borrowed or purchased through normal channels. Sometimes old copies are available but are very expensive. Another source for these now is:XEROX UNIVERSITY MICROFILMS, 300 Seeb Rd., Ann Arbor, MI 48106. Xerox University Microfilms has quite an impressive list of books for which they have prepared copies. They are continually adding to the list and will attempt to get a copy of almost any out of print book for you, if you will pay the price and can supply the location and bibliographic data.

One of the earliest of colonial institutions was the "Town Meeting". All affairs of the local community were aired at these meetings, and minutes were recorded. At one time or another almost everyone who lived in the community had their name mentioned for one reason or another. These old records, where still existing, have been microfilmed by the Genealogical Society of the LDS Church, and are in the library at Salt Lake City,UT. If you have reason to believe that an ancestor lived in a particular town, but have been unable to find a record in the vital statistics, or church records, a check of the Town Meeting Records might prove helpful.

Having mentioned above, the Genealogical Society of the LDS Church, a few further words of explanation are probably necessary at this time. The finest genealogical library anywhere is the Family History Library of the Chuirch of Jesus Christ of Latter Day Saints (Mormon) in Salt Lake City, UT. It has on microfilm not only records from all over the United States but from throughout the world. There is on microfilm the equivalent of more than 4 million books of 300 pages each. There are many records from Ireland and these will be discussed further in the next chapter. The records do not only cover LDS Church members but persons of all faiths and of no faith. While these records were originally gathered by the LDS Church for the use of its members in performing genealogical research which is a part of their religious practice, they do not limit the use of the library to only their own members. All persons, regardless of their religious preference, are welcome to use the library in Salt Lake City or any of the Branch Libraries throughout the country. In the next chapter there will be a discussion of how you may access these records.

After you have gathered all of the information that you can from family memberes and from other easily accessible records, one of the methods to follow is to check the indexes. While an index will not give you complete information, if they do give a reference to an ancestor, they can save you hours of time and effort by directing your search in more fruitful directions. Among the indexes and general reference works that can be used, and which are found in most large libraries, are the ones listed here:

"American and British Genealogy and Heraldry",P. William Filby, compiler. Secod Edition, Chicago:American Library Assn. 1975.

"American Genealogical Index", Fremont Rider, Editor. Middletown,CT 1942-52.

"American Genealogical-Biographical Index to American Genealogical and Local History Materials", Fremont Rider, Editor. Middletown,CT.

"Annual Index to Genealogical Periodicals and Family Histories", compiled by Inez Waldermaier. Volumes for 1957-63.

"Genealogical Periodical Annual Index". Vols. 1-4. Edited by Ellen S. Rogers. Covers 1962-65. Bladensburg, MD. Volumes 5-8. Covers 1963-67. Edited by George Russell, Mitchell, MD. Later years edited by Laird C. Towle. Available from HERITAGE BOOKS, Bowie, MD.

"Index to American Genealogies", 5th edition Revised. Albany, NY:Joel Munsell and Sons, 1900, 1908. Reprint-Genealogical Publishing Co., Baltimore, MD.

"Index to Genealogical Periodicals". Donald L. Jacobus. Covers 1932-53. Reprint: Genealogical Publishing Co., Baltimore, MD.

"NewEngland Historic Genealogical Register Index", Vols. 1-50. Originally published by New England Historic Genealogical Society. Reprint: Genealogical Publishing Co., Baltimore, MD. Volumes 51-102 of above compiled by Gertrude S. Wright.

"A General Index to a Census of Pensioners for Revolutionary or Military Service". 1840. Prepared by Genealogical Society, LDS Church. Reprint: Genealogical Publishing Co., Baltimore, MD.

"The Compendium of American Genealogy". Frederick Adams Virkus. 7 Volumes. (The most complete collection of lineages of the first families of America.) Published by Genealogical Publishing Co., Baltimore, MD.

"American Ancestry", Joel Munsell and Sons. 12 Volumes. (A virtual Who's Who of colonial families.)Reprint: Genealogical Publishing Co., Baltimore, MD.

Another very important source of genealogical information is in the Federal Land Records. Some states will search these records for you, if you can identify the county and township. This information is sometimes difficult to obtain. However, if you are interested in someone whom you think purchased land from the United States government between 1789 and 1839, there is a publication that will help. It is "Grass Roots of America-An Index to the American State Papers, Land Grants and Claims, 1789-1839". It covers the states of Alabama, Arkansas, Florida, Georgia, Illinois, Indiana, Iowa, Michigan, Minnesota, Mississippi, Missouri and Wisconsin.This index was made from the Gales and Seaton publication of the American State Papers in the 1800's. One copy is in the Library of Congress and another is in the University of Utah Library. Only 750 copies were printed but it is possible to find it in some large libraries.

Much information may be found in old newspapers, particularly in the form of birth, death and marriage notices. To find if there was a newspaper in the area at the time in question, you may wish to consult"The Union List of Newspapers, 1821-1936" by Winfield Gregory. This is available at major libraries. It lists the newspapers still available from the period 1821 to 1936 and where they may be found.

There are many specialized publications which may be of help to the Scotch-Irish researcher. One example of such a publication is, "Archives of the Pioneers of Tazewell County Virginia".This contains over 30,000 references to official records. It covers all or part of eight present day counties in Virginia and West Virginia. A county of 200 years ago covered the area of several of todays counties. This book is available from: NETTI SCHREINER-YANTIS, 6818 Lois Drive, Springfield, VA 22150. This book is mentioned here because of an unusual feature. Ms. Yantis will provide an index list of persons mentioned in the book, prior to your purchasing it. This gives the prospective buyer the opportunity to determine if he should buy this book rather than some other one. Ms. Yantis also has available a number of other books of interest covering areas of Virginia. One of these is "Montgomery County, Virginia Circa 1790". In 1790 Montgomery County covered all or parts of 22 counties of present day VA and WV. Another publication available from Ms. Yantis is "Genealogical Books in Print". This lists genealogical books and periodicals available throughout the United States, including source, address and price. There are a number of editions. Look for it in your local library or write to address above.

Among some of the other many helpful books are:

"Pennsylvania Genealogies: Chiefly Scotch-Irish and German" by William Egle. This has 1500 surnames in its 24 page index.

"Chronicles of the Scotch-Irish Settlement in Virginia, extracted from the Original Court Records of Augusta County, 1745-1800", by Lyman Chalkey, Three Volumes, Rosslyn,VA 1912.

"Scotch-Irish in America: Proceedings and Addreesses of the Congress", Volumes 1-8, by the Scotch-Irish Society of America, 1889-96.

Probably anyone who is interested in researching their Scotch-Irish ancestry, might have some interest in the "Scotch-Irish Society". Here is the address to which you may write for particulars about joining or about how they might help you in your research.

Scotch-Irish Society of the U.S.
13 Thompson Drive
Havertown, PA 19083

At this point, particularly if you have located the town, townland or county in Ireland from which your immigrant ancestor came, a good map of Ireland would be helpful. Most of the maps that you will find in the atlases in the public library do not give the detail needed to locate very small villages. Irish travel maps with sufficient detail are available from Genealogy Unlimited, Inc., P.O. Box 537, Orem, UT 84059. Write to them for prices. Some of the maps are scaled 4 miles to the inch so there is a lot of detail. The very detailed maps split Ireland into five sections, so be sure to specify the particular county or counties in which you are interestred.

CHAPTER IV

ANCESTOR HUNTING IN NORTHERN IRELAND

We assume that by this time you may have located the name of the town or townland, or at least the county in Ireland, from which your Scotch-Irish ancestors emigrated. If you haven't, all is not lost, as we will explain further on in this chapter.

Beginers in Irish research often hear about the difficulties with the lack of records. Quite often the lack of records is attributed to the fire that took place in the Public Record Office of Ireland during the civil war in 1922. The civil war occurred between the "Treaty" and "Anti-Treaty" forces. That is between those who were agreeing with the treaty to set up the Irish Free State and thereby partition Ireland and those who were opposed to partition. While many records were lost in the fire, many have been replaced from other sources. The real lack of records is caused by the fact that they never existed for the majority of the Irish people. Records for the Catholic majority just were not kept during the time of the Penal Codes.

Anyone wishing to do research in Ireland either Scotch-Irish or native Irish needs to have an understanding of the political and administrative divisions of Ireland, and particularly that political unit now known as Northern Ireland. It is important to keep in mind that Ireland was not divided prior to 1922. Until that time all records for all of Ireland were kept in Dublin. After the establishment of Northern Ireland copies of the records pertaining to the six counties that constitute Northern Ireland are kept in Belfast. More on this later.

All record keeping in Ireland, as in most countries, was done by political or administrative division of the land. Some understanding of these administrative units, and their changes throughout the years is necessary to understand records in any part of Ireland.

Early Ireland was divided into five kingdoms. One of these, the Kingdom of Meath was merged with Leinster to become the Province of Leinster, one of the historic four provinces of Ireland. The other three provinces are Ulster, Munster and Connaught.

After the Norman invasion, the English introduced the "shire" or county sysem to Ireland. The first twelve counties were established in 1210 by King John. Additional counties were established until the last, Wicklow, was divided from Dublin in 1605. All of Ireland, since 1605, has been divided into thirty-two counties. After the partition in 1922, six of the nine counties of Ulster became known as Northern Ireland and remained with the Crown, outside of the Irish Free State. The Republic of Ireland, as formed in 1949, consists of the 26 counties which formed the Irish Free

State in 1922. All of the Provinces of Munster, Leinster and Connaught are in the Republic, as are three of the counties of Ulster. The following shows the arrangement of counties within each province:

REPUBLIC OF IRELAND

LEINSTER	MUNSTER	CONNAUGHT	ULSTER
Carlow	Clare	Galway	Cavan
Dublin	Cork	Leitrim	Donegal
Kilkenny	Kerry	Mayo	Monaghan
Kildare	Limerick	Roscommon	
Longford	Tipperary	Sligo	
Louth	Waterford		
Meath			
Offaly(King's)			
Westmeath			
Wexford			
Wicklow			
Laois(Queen's)			

NORTHERN IRELAND

ULSTER
Antrim
Armagh
Down
Fermanagh
Derry(formerly Coleraine)
Tyronne

During the 17th Century, a number of national surveys, some of which will be discussed later, were made on a county basis. The county was an important unit in the administration of the various plantation schemes of the 17th Century, which included the plantation of Scots into Ulster and the transplantation of the native Irish from their confiscated lands to new and poorer lands beyond the Shannon. The counties of Ireland were mapped by Sir William Petty in 1654 in what is known as the Down Survey. The map's of Petty's were the standard maps of Ireland until the current Ordnance Survey maps of Ireland were completed. Figure 13 shows the counties of Ulster as they exist today, three of them in the Republic, and six in Northern Ireland.

The "barony" is another administrative unit used by the English as a unit of land ownership. Each barony may have consisted originally of the land of one or more of the Irish septs or clans. Data in a number of land surveys of the 17th Century was collected on a barony basis. The "Books of Survey and Distribution", which summarize changes in land ownership after the Cromwellian

NORTHERN IRELAND

A. Antrim
B. Armaagh
C. Down
D. Fermanagh
E. Derry (formerly Coleraine)
F. Tyronne

REPUBLIC OF IRELAND (Eire)

1. Cavan
2. Donegal
3. Monoghan

THE COUNTIES OF ULSTER

FIGURE 13

confiscations (circa 1660), referred to the baronies. The barony was used as a census division up to 1901. By that time, however, the barony was no longere a meaningful territorial division.

Figure 14 lists the various baronies in each of the nine counties of Ulster. There is some duplication of names of baronies in some of the counties not listed here. This requires some care in identification in your later research. Be certain the record you are scanning or requesting for a particular barony is also identified by the correct county.

In addition to the Civil Provinces of Ulster, Leinster, Munster and Connaught, Ireland was also divided into Ecclesiastical Provinces. These religious divisions were Armagh, Tuam, Dublin and Cashel. The Ecclesiastical Provinces were further divided into dioceses, and these in turn into parishes, as an administrative unit for record keeping. The difficulty came because of the ever changing status of the parish. Parishes in Ireland were, as elsewhere, the smallest administrative unit of the Catholic Church. When the Anglo-Normans arrived, they were familiar with the parochial system and did not change it, although they did rename some of the parishes to give them names of more universally recognized saints. When the Reformation came, and the English extended it into Ireland with the establishment of the Church of Ireland, the administrative system of the Catholic Church was disrupted. The old administrative dioceses were adopted by the Protestant Church of Ireland. The diocese were also adopted by the English as civil territorial divisions in some of the land surveys. The diocese are shown on the map in Figure 15. Published wills are usually identified by Ecclesiastical Province and Diocese.

A book entitled"Topographical Dictionary of Ireland", by Samuel Lewis(1837) is very useful in relating townland and civil parishes to Catholic Unions as the Catholic Parishes were later called. This book has recently been reprinted in the United States. It is expensive since it is a sizeable book. It can be found in the reference section of many large public and university libraries.

The English civil parishes were based upon the original Catholic Parishes. Since the Catholic Parishes all but disappeared in the 17th and 18th Centuries, and Church of Ireland Parishes with different boundaries were established, there can be much confusion as to parish identification. The Civil Parishes have no relationship to today's parishes, either Catholic or Protestant. The Civil Parish boundaries were marked in the early Ordnance Survey maps and they were used as Census Divisions as well as divisions in the Primary Evaluation of Tenants in 1850. A list of all of the civil parishes in Northern Ireland is shown in Figure 16, 16A and 16B.

BARONIES OF THE THREE COUNTIES OF ULSTER IN THE REPUBLIC OF IRELAND

1.CAVAN
Tullyhaw
Lower Loughter
Upper Loughter
Tullygarry
Clankee
Castlerahan
Clanmahon
Tullyhunco

2.DONEGAL
Kilmacreena
East Inishowen
West Inishowen
Boylagh
Tirhugh
Rapahoe North
Rapahoe South
Banagh

3.MONOGHAN
Trough
Monaghan
Dartree
Cremorne
Farney

BARONIES OF THE SIX COUNTIES OF ULSTER IN NORTHERN IRELAND

A. ANTRIM
Cary
Lower Dunluce
Upper Dunluce
Kilconway
Lower Glenmarm
Upper Glenmarm
Lower Toome
Upper Toome
Lower Antrim
Upper Antrim
Lower Belfast
Upper Belfast
Lower Massereene
Upper Massereene
Carrickfergus

B. ARMAGH
O'Neilland East
O'Neilland West
Armagh
Lower Fews
Upper Fews
Tirrany
Lower Orior
Upper Orior

C. DOWN
Lower Ards
Upper Ards
Lower Castlereigh
Upper Castlereigh
Lower Iveagh(Upper-half)
Lower Iveagh(Lower-half)
Upper Iveagh(Upper-half)
Lower Iveagh(Lower-half)
Lower Lecale
Upper Lecale
Kinelarty
Mourne
Newry

D. FERMANAGH
Lurg
Maghevaboy
Tirkennedy
Clamawley
Knockninny
Coole
Clankelly
Magnerastephane

E. DERRY
Tirkeeran
Keenaght
Coleraine
Loughinsholin

F. TYRONNE
West Omagh
East Omagh
Lower Strabane
Upper Strabane
Upper Dungannon
Middle Dungannon
Lower Dungannon
Clogher

THE BARONIES OF THE PROVINCE OF ULSTER

FIGURE 14

THE ECCLESIASTICAL DIOCESE OF IRELAND

FIGURE 15

THE PARISHES OF COUNTY ANTRIM

1 Aghagallon
2 Aghalee
3 Ahoghill
4 Antrim
5 Ardclinis
6 Armoy
7 Ballinderry
8 Ballintoy
9 Ballyclug
10 Ballycor
11 Ballylinny
12 Ballymartin
13 Ballymoney
14 Ballynure
15 Ballyrashane
16 Ballyscullion
17 Ballywillin
18 Belfast
19 Billy
20 Blaris
21 Camlin
22 Carncastle
23 Carnmoney
24 Carrickfergus
25 Connor
26 Craigs
27 Cranfield
28 Culfeightrin
29 Derryaghy
30 Derrykeighan
31 Donegore
32 Drumbeg
33 Drummaul
34 Dunaghy
35 Duneane
36 Dunluce
37 Finvoy
38 Glenavy
39 Glenwherry
40 Glynn
41 Grange of Ballyscullion
42 Grange of Doagh
43 Grange of Drumtullagh
44 Grange of Dundermot
45 Grange of Inispollen
46 Grange of Killyglen
47 Grange of Layd
48 Grange of Muckamore
49 Grange of Nilteen
50 Grange of Shilvodan
51 Inver
52 Island Magee
53 Kilbride
54 Killagan
55 Killead
56 Kilraghts
57 Kilroots
58 Kilwaughter
59 Kirkinriola
60 Lambeg
61 Larne
62 Layd
63 Loughguile
64 Magheragall
65 Maghermesk
66 Newton Crommlin
67 Portglenone
68 Racavan
69 Raloo
70 Ramoan
71 Rasharkin
72 Rashee
73 Rathlin
74 Shankill
75 Skerry
76 Templecorran
77 Templepatrick
78 Tickmacrevan
79 Tullyrusk

THE PARISHES OF COUNTY ARMAGH

1 Armagh
2 Ballymore
3 Ballymyre
4 Clonfeacle
5 Creggan
6 Derrynoose
7 Drumcree
8 Eglish
9 Forkill
10 Grange
11 Jonesborough
12 Keady
13 Kilclooney
14 Kildarton
15 Kilevy
16 Killyman
17 Kilmore
18 Lisnadill
19 Loughgall
20 Loughgilly
21 Magheralin
22 Montiaghs
23 Mullaghbrack
24 Newry
25 Newtownhamilton
26 Seagoe
27 Shankill
28 Tartyaraghan
29 Tynan

FIGURE 16

THE PARISHES OF COUNTY DOWN

1 Aghaderg
2 Annaclone
3 Annahilt
4 Ardglass
5 Ardkeen
6 Ardquin
7 Ballee
8 Ballyculter
9 Ballyhalbert alias St. Andrew
10 Ballykinler
11 Ballyphilip
12 Ballytrustan
13 Ballywalter
14 Bangor
15 Blaris
16 Bright
17 Castleboy
18 Clonallan
19 Clonduff
20 Comber
21 Donaghadee
22 Donaghcloney
23 Donaghmore
24 Down
25 Dromara
26 Dromore
27 Drumballyroney
28 Drumbeg
29 Drumbo
30 Drumgath
31 Drumgooland
32 Dundonald
33 Dunsfort
34 Garvaghy
35 Grey Abbey
36 Hillsborough
37 Holywood
38 Inch
39 Inishargy
40 Kilbroney
41 Kilclief
42 Kilcoo
43 Kilkeel
44 Killaney
45 Killinchy
46 Killyleagh
47 Kilmegan
48 Kilmood
49 Kilmore
50 Knockbreda
51 Lambeg
52 Loughinisland
53 Maghera
54 Magheradrool
55 Magherahamlet
56 Magheralin
57 Magherally
58 Moira
59 Newry
60 Newtownards
61 Rathmullan
62 Saintfield
63 Saul
64 Seapatrick
65 Shankill
66 Slanes
67 Tullyfish
68 Tullynakill
69 Tyrella
70 Warrenpoint

THE PARISHES OF COUNTY TYRONE

1 Aghaloo
2 Aghalurcher
3 Arboe
4 Ardstraw
5 Artrea
6 Ballinderry
7 Ballyclog
8 Bodoney Lower
9 Bodoney Upper
10 Camus
11 Cappagh
12 Carnteel
13 Clogher
14 Clogherny
15 Clonfeacle
16 Clonoe
17 Derryloran
18 Desertcreat
19 Donacavey
20 Donaghedy
21 Donaghenry
22 Donaghmore
23 Dromore
24 Drumglass
25 Drumragh
26 Errigal Keerogue
27 Errigal Trough
28 Kildress
29 Killeeshill
30 Killyman
31 Kilskerry
32 Learmount
33 Leckpatrick
34 Lissan
35 Longfield East
36 Longfield West
37 Magheracross
38 Pomeroy
39 Tamlaght
40 Termonamongan
41 Termonmaguirk
42 Tullyniskan
43 Urney

FIGURE 16A

THE PARISHES OF COUNTY DERRY

1 Aghadowney
2 Aghanloo
3 Agivey
4 Arboe
5 Artrea
6 Ballinderry
7 Ballyaghran
8 Ballymoney
9 Ballynascreen
10 Ballyrashane
11 Ballyscullion
12 Ballywillin
13 Balteagh
14 Banagher
15 Bovevagh
16 Carrick
17 Clondermot
18 Coleraine
19 Cumber Lower
20 Cumber Upper
21 Derryloran
22 Desertlyn
23 Desertmartin
24 Desertoghill
25 Drumachose
26 Dunboe
27 Dungiven
28 Errigal
29 Faughanvale
30 Formoyle
31 Kilcronaghan
32 Kildollagh
33 Killelagh
34 Killowen
35 Killrea
36 Learmount
37 Lissan
38 Macosquin
39 Maghera
40 Magherafelt
41 Tamlaght
42 Tamlaght Finlagan
43 Tamlaght O'Crilly
44 Tamlaghyard
45 Templemore
46 Termoneeny

THE PARISHES OF COUNTY FERMANAGH

1 Aghalurcher
2 Aghavea
3 Belleek
4 Boho
5 Clones
6 Cleenish
7 Derrybrusk
8 Derryvullan
9 Devenish
10 Drumkeeran
11 Drummully
12 Enniskillen
13 Galloon
14 Inishmacsaint
15 Killesher
16 Kinawley
17 Magheracross
18 Magheraculmoney
19 Rossorry
20 Templecarn
21 Tomregan
22 Trory

FIGURE 16B

The "townland" is the smallest administrative division in the county, and its main purpose is to distinguish between different locations. The townland does not necessarily include a settled village or town. Some are entirely farmland. The nearest counterpart to the townland in the United States would be the township structure of counties in the Midwest. Petty in his survey (1654) divided baronies and parishes into townlands. The townland became the basic division of the county in the 17th Century. The association of the townland with land ownership dates from that period. From that time on, land was let by landlords on a townland basis and townland names were recorded in a variety of documents concerning land.

There are approximately 60,000 townlands in all of Ireland, with slightly more than 9,300 of them in Northern Ireland. Some of them cross parish or even county boundaries. When this occurs, it is best to check the records of both parishes to be certain to get the correct information. The names of townlands are not unique. There is much duplication. Some townlands have the same names as baronies. Some differ only by having the prefix "Upper" or "Lower". In some cases the townland name is the same as a county name in another part of Ireland. If this sounds confusing, it should serve to emphasize the need to clearly identify the location of a townland, with a barony and/or parish and county.

Detailed maps of 19th Century Ireland, which will closely resemble 17th Century Ireland are available in "The Genealogical Atlas of Ireland" published by Deseret Book Co. Salt Lake City, UT. The maps are from two sources:Samuel Lewis "Atlas of the Counties of Ireland", published in 1846, and George Phillips'"Handy Atlas of the Counties of Ireland", published in 1885. The "Genealogical Atlas" also contains a gazetteer which lists all of the towns and villages shown on the maps. This book is valuable in locating places in Ireland both in Northern Ireland and in the Republic of Ireland.

As stated earlier, in 1922 at the formation of the Irish Free State which preceded the Republic, three of the nine counties of Ulster, namely Cavan, Donegal and Monaghan chose to become a part of the Irish Free State. Cavan and Donegal had a considerable settlement of Scots. If it happens that your research determines that your Scotch-Irish ancestor came from Cavan or Donegal, you will have to continue your search in Dublin in the Public Record Office there. Several other counties which are now in the Republic also had settlers from King James' plantations, but these were primarily English rather than Scots.

Prior to 1920 the records from all local and county departments and courts were sent to Dublin for storage in the Public Record Office (PRO), which is in a building called the Four Courts. It was this building which was shelled during the

Irish Civil War, starting a fire which resulted in some loss of records.

The British Parliament passed the Government of Ireland Act in 1920. This established the Irish Free State and Northern Ireland. It was not actually effective until 1922. In the following year, 1923, the Northern Ireland government established its own Public Record Office to house the records currently being generated in the six counties. Because of the turbulent times, a number of records hadn't been sent to Dublin during some of the years preceding partition. It would have been possible to treat this new office as only one to house the 20th Century records being accumulated. However, since so many records were destroyed in the Dublin fire, attempts were made both north and south to replace them from various sources. The newly appointed Deputy Keeper of the Northern Ireland Public Record Office (PRONI) had a keen sense of history and the good fortune of having on his staff two employees who had worked in the Dublin Public Record Office (PRO) where he also had worked before partition. This new office, the PRONI, started out with offices on the fourth floor of the Linen Handerchief Company on Murray Street in Belfast. In 1933 the office moved to new quarters in the Law Courts Building. By this time many older records had been obtained from a variety of sources. A very good account of how these records were accumulated can be found in "Irish Historical Studies" Volume 8, 1952. It is written by Mr. D.A. Chart, who was the first Deputy Keeper of the PRONI.

While the PRONI concentrates mainly on records for the six counties, they have acquired along the way, some very old and complete records concerning areas in the Republic of Ireland. The PRO in Dublin also continues to keep those records it has on the six counties prior to 1922(which weren't destroyed in the fire.)

In the systematic replacement of records from other sources, the PRO occassionally gets new records on Ulster as well. While there was never any official transfer of records from one government to another, there has been a tremendous cooperation between the Public Record Offices of the two governments. While each keeps its own records, each is aware of the needs of the other and makes copies available, whenever they come upon records that would be valuable to the other office.

The address of the PRONI is as follows:

Public Record Office of Northern Ireland
66 Balmoral Ave.
Belfast, BT9 6NY
Northern Ireland U.K.

The search room is open to the public each day, Monday to

Friday, from 9.30a.m. to 4.45p.m., and for a nominal fee the researcher has at their disposal the greatest collection of genealogical and historical information available anywhere on Northern Ireland. Unfortunately, not all of us can travel to Belfast to do the research personally, and in recent years, Belfast has not been particularly inviting to tourists. The personnel of PRONI do not perform research, either for persons visiting or for those writing to them. They are helpful to visitors in showing them the general system and in helping to locate particular materials. Visitors who wish to have research done for them, or written inquiries, are turned over to the Ulster Historical Foundation which is at the same location. It was formerly called the Ulster-Scot Historical Foundation. The address is:

Ulster Historical Foundation
66 Balmoral Ave.
Belfast, BT9 6NY
Northern Ireland,U.K.

In writing to the foundation, include one or two International Reply Coupons, depending whether you wish a reply by surface mail or air mail. International Reply Coupons (IRC's) are available at most post offices in the United States. You send these instead of the usual SASE.

To start an inquiry regarding one or more Ulster families, write to the Foundation and request an application form. When this is received, fill it out as completely as possible.It must be returned with a registration fee. The application form states the rates and conditions for research by the Foundation.

It seems it would be possible to stop right here and say, from this point on, put all of your resaearch into the hands of the Ulster Historical Foundation. This would probably, eventually, get the job done, but the family genealogist missesmuch of the fun if they do not in some way participate in the search. To do this you need to know more about the kind of records available and also other sources of help so that you can make choices on how to proceed.

There are two books which have recently been published which are of interest to researchers in Ireland including the six counties of Northern Ireland. The books are:

A Guide to Irish Parish Registers
by Brian Mitchell, 151 pp.
Genealogical Publishing Co.
1001 N, Calvert St,
Baltimore, MD 21202

Irish Records-Sources for Family and Local History
by James G. Ryan, 562 pp.
Ancestry, Inc.
P.O. Box 476
Salt Lake City, UT 84110

In 1981 a new organization was founded to provide help in researching families of both Scotch-Irish and Gaelic- Irish backgrounds, along with the Anglo-Irish who are sometimes inter-related with both groups.This new organization is the:

Irish Genealogical Association
164 Kingsway, Dunmurry,
Belfast, BT17 9AD
Northern Ireland U.K.

Write to them for details of their services, which include not only research but publication of a fine magazine called "Irish Family Links". The Association is a private group and has no government support. It is funded entirely by its members fees, etc. The Association has organized several gatherings of Irish and Scotch-Irish Clans over the past few years. They also publish an inexpensive handbook entitled "How to Trace Family History in Northern Ireland" by Kathleen Neill, the founder of the Association.

Earlier it was mentioned that we would explain how to access the many records of the LDS Family History Library. Practically all of the Irish and Scotch-Irish Records dscussed in this book are available for viewing at the LDS (Mormon) Family History Library or at any of its many Family History Centers (formerly called Branch Libraries) throughout the United States. While each branch does not have all of the books, they do have the card catalog of the Salt Lake City library on microfilm. You check the microfilm catalog for the book or record that you want and tell one of the library volunteers. They then order the book or record from Salt Lake City. You will have to pay a small fee to cover the cost of shipping and handling. You will be notified when the film arrives at the local Family History Center so that you may go back there and check the records for yourself. You can usually tell if there is an LDS Family History Center in your city or a nearby one by checking the telephone book.. Look in your local telephone book under "Churches" for the "Church of Jesus Christ of Latter Day Saints". If the library is not mentioned, call the church office and ask where the nearest Family History Center is located. As mentioned in the previous chapter, these libraries are open to all, regardless of religious preference. The author is not of the LDS (Mormon) faith, but has used two different Branch Libraries on numerous occassions. The volunteers who staff the library will make you feel welcome and assist you in getting started to use this wonderful resource. Don't hesitate to use it.

Another method for checking records in the LDS Family History Library is to hire a record researcher. A number of them advertise in the GENEALOGICAL HELPER. Some are students at Brigham Young University in nearby Provo, UT. The rates are usually reasonable. Determine through correspondence the searchers rate per hour. Send enough money as an advance for several hours of research time. Place a limit on how much time should be spent searching before reporting back to you. On the basis of the report that you get you can determine if you wish to send more money for additional search time. Keep in mind that you must direct the search, that is tell which records you want searched. A record searcher is just that, not a genealogist who will organize and direct the search. Such services cost more.

Usually we assume that you have discovered the name of the townland or at least the county of origin of your immigrant ancestor, from your search of American records. Some will not be able to do this, so there are several methods to work with if you happen to be one of the unlucky people who still haven't located the ancestral county. The first source to check is a book entitled"A Census of Ireland-Circa 1659" edited by Seamus Pender and published by the Irish Manuscript Commission. It is available in many large public and university libraries. If your local library does not have it, they can get it on Inter-Library Loan. This is one of the few early census reports available for all of Ireland. Remember at that time all 32 counties were one country. The returns are listed geographically by county, barony, parish and townland. Searching through each of the counties of Ulster is not a particularly big job, and it is almost certain to turn up your ancestors. Even if you don't have the specific name, you will find persons of the surname. If you check the nine counties of Ulster without success, try checking some of the other counties bordering on Ulster.Since we know that the earliest arrivals among the Scots were about 1607 and that the migration to America didn't start until about 1717, this census being about half way in between , makes it a likely list to turn up relatives who were planters.

Another method used to determine a location for an ancestor will work only if some of the people of that surname stayed in Ireland. Of course, not all Scotch-Irish emigrated. This method uses the "Special Report on Surnames of Ireland". This was produced by the Registrar General's Office in 1894. It is based upon the 1890 census. It reports the number of births that year for each surname and then lists the names of the counties in which county there were at least five births of that surname. Using this method along with Griffith's Evaluation, which will be discussed in the next pararagraph, you may be able to refine the process of locating the area in which to search for your ancestors. That is, of course, unless you have already located their place of origin in Ulster. The list of surnames mentioned above is published in a book entitled,"Irish Ancestors", by Michael O'Laughlin. The publisher is:

Irish Genealogical Foundation
P.O.Box 7575
Kansas City, MO 64116

In the mid-1800's there was a general survey of land values for the purpose of local taxation. The full name of the survey was "Griffith's Primary Valuation of Tenements, 1848-64". It is usually just referred to as Griffith's Valuation. It fills over 200 volumesefor each barony. It contains the name of each property holder, his townland or street address, the name of his immediate landlord, if any, a description of his holding as well as details of the valuation.All of the surnames in Grffith's Valuation have been indexed in a book entitled "An Index of Surnames in Griffith's Primary Evaluation and Tithe Applotment Books". There is a separate book for each county, and then within the county, the listing is by barony. After each surname listed, there is printed the letter G and a number. This number indicates the number of times that surname occurs in that barony in Griffith's Valuation. If the surname also occurred in that barony in another survey, "The Tithe Applotment Book", the letter "T" is also indicated after the surname. This information, then, can be used in conjunction with that listed above to determine in which counties and baronies to search. It is not foolproof but it does offer a good chance of success if no other sources have determined the place of origin of your ancestor.

There are extensive manuscript collections available in the PRONI, each with pedigrees of individual families. You can inquire of the Ulster Historical Foundation if they have a manuscript or pedigree on the particular family in which you are interested. You can also find a list of 848 of these pedigrees in Margaret Falley's monumental work "Irish and Scotch-Irish Ancestral Research", which is available at most large public libraries. If it is not in the library in your city, they can get it for you on Inter-Library Loan as explained in Chapter III. There are two volumes of the book. The Dewey Call Number is 929.1415. This book may also be purchased from GENEALOGICAL PUBLISHING CO., 1001 N. Calvert St., Baltimore, MD 21202. If the PRONI has a family manuscript collection for the name in which you are interested, they will supply copies for a fee. For example, there are 3 different Alexander family manuscripts and 5 for Andrews.

In addition to the wealth of information at the Public Record Office of Northern Ireland which is available to researchers, there are other fine sources of information. Since most of the Scotch-Irish were Presbyterian while in Ireland, much information is available in the Library of the Presbyterian Historical Society in Belfast. The library is not open to the public but they have in the past answered specific written inquiries. The address is:

Presbyterian Historical Society
Church House, Room 20
Fisherwick Place
Belfast, Northern Ireland

Of the 367 Presbyterian congregations in Ireland, 82 of them are located in the Republic of Ireland. This means 285 of them are in Northern Ireland. Of these 249 have retained custody of their church registers. Thirty-six of the very old registers are stored in the vault of the Presbyterian Historical Society.

It is possible to get the name of the present minister of any Presbyterian congregation in Ireland by writing to the Presbyterian Historical Society. You can then write directly to the minister requesting a search of the records. In each case a gratuity should be included to cover the cost of the time the minister will spend checking records for you. In writing to the minister, it would be well to ask if there is any additional cost over and above the amount sent, or for further researh if it is recommended.

The Presbyterian Historical Society, a number of years ago, issued three pamphlets written by the Reverend David Stewart. These contain valuable lists of the Scots who settled in Ulster, mainly in the reign of James I. These pamphlets list the settlers alphabetically by county. Please inquire of the society as to availability and price of these lists.

While most Scotch-Irish immigrants were Presbyterian, do not overlook the Church of Ireland Records as a possible source of information. Beause of political expediency, many Presbyterians, as well as Roman Catholics, bowed to the pressure and conformed to the Church of Ireland. In Irish research it is always well to check the Church of Ireland records, particularly when records cannot be found elsewhere. This is true regardless of what religion we may thought the ancestor to have been. The PRONI has copies of about 116 of the roughly 250 Church of Ireland Registers in Northern Ireland.

The Representative Church Body of the Church of Ireland is making a new effort aimed at replacing those Church Registers lost in the 1922 fire. They have made some progress and since this is an on going effort, they expect to make much more in the future. To contact them, write to:

Representative Church Body Library
Church of Ireland
Braemor Park, Rathgar,
Dublin, IRELAND

The names of the cities and towns of Ulster have changed little over the past 300 years and are to be found on most detailed maps of Ireland. There is a book entitled, "Topographical Index of Northern Ireland" which was published with the Census of Northern Ireland in 1927. This contains tables listing every barony, parish, town and townland. The lists place every town in its proper parish along with the townlands included in it. This can be somewhat confusing since now some of the towns can encompass several townlands. This book was reprinted in 1947.

Copies of deeds, leases, wills, marriage settlements, etc. for all counties of Ireland, both North and South, for the years prior to 1922, are at the Registry of Deeds on Henrietta Street in Dublin. It was established in 1708. If you have the opportunity to visit Dublin and are interested in genealogy, or in land records in general, you should not miss a visit to the Registry of Deeds. If you have only a limited time to spend you probably won't find much in the way of needed information, but you should still make the visit. The Registry of Deeds is in what was called the King's Inn, a rather imposing monument to the days of English rule. On the first floor there is the bustling activity of local solicitors and clerks engaged in checking and recorded present day transactions. The older records are on the second floor and genealogists are permitted to search these old records. Once you make it known that you are interested in the old records for genealogical purposes, you'll be ushered to the second floor. There, the system of Names Indexes and Place or Land Indexes and the general layout of the records will be explained to you. Then you are on your own. Depending upon the time of day and other factors, there may be no one else around. Possibly there may be one or two other searchers in the adjacent room. These very large volumes have records going back to the early 1700's and here you find yourself in a setting reminiscent of Charles Dickens - a high desk or table, a high stool and yourself pouring over almost iillegible transactions of the 1700-1800's.

If you cannot go to Dublin to check the records, you need only miss the atmosphere. You can still get the information.The names Indexes have been put on 123 reels of microfilm. The Land Indexes are on 283 rolls. All of the microfilm is in the LDS Family History Library in Salt Lake City, UT. Again, you can have a record searcher in Salt Lake check these records for you or you can do it yourself at a Family History Center near your home. Remember these are only Indexes on the microfilm.

However, if you find a record that appears to be of interest, you can make a note of the reference numbers and order a copy of the document from the Registry of Deeds, Henrietta Street, Dublin, Republic of Ireland.

A detailed article concerning the Registry of Deeds by Miss Rosemary ffolliott appears in the March 1975 issue of the Genealogical Journal of the Utah Genealogical Society. Miss ffolliott is an experienced researcher in all of Irish records, having worked at one time for the Genealogical Office in Dublin. She is the editor of a periodical entitled "The Irish Ancestor". Write for current price and ordering information to:

Miss Rosemary ffolliott
The Glebe House,
Fethard, County Tipperary
REPUBLIC OF IRELAND

A list of the various volumes of the Index to the Registry of Deeds appears in Margaret Falley's work, cited earlier.

The Probate Records or records of wills can provide a lot of genealogical information. From 1536 to 1858 all wills were probated or proved by the ecclesiastical courts of the Church of Ireland, regardless of the religion of the individual making the will. In 1858 the jurisdiction passed to the civil courts throughout Ireland.

Many of the wills were lost in the Four Courts fire of 1922.The Indexes to the wills, however, were not destroyed because they happened to have been removed to another building, for some reason, just before the fire. A number of Indexes to Irish Wills have been published. Among the more popular are: "Index to the Prerogative Wills of Ireland, 1536-1810", by Sir Arthur Vicars, and the five volume set referred to as the "Phillimore Indexes to Irish Wills". These were edited by W.P.W. Phillimore(Vol. I & II) and Gertrude Thrift (Vol. III, IV and V). This is probably the most comprehensive publication of indexes to Irish wills. It can be found in many genealogical and public libraries. There are a number of other published indexes. Many of these indexes are listed in Margaret Falley's work.

If a particular name in the Index of Wills is of interest to you, you should know that Sir William Bethan once filled 241 notebooks with pedigrees copied from these wills. His collection is in the PRO. The address of the PRO is:

Public Record Office
Four Courts Bldg.
Dublin, Republic of Ireland

Many other Irish records and genealogical information in

general from both the North and the South of Ireland can be had from:

The Chief Herald
Genealogical Office
Kildare Street
Dublin, Republic of Ireland

As mentioned earlier the Registry of Deeds began in 1708. Therefore, it would not show any original deeds of the early Scot planters. The "Civil Survey 1654-56" is a listing of the proprietors of land essentially as it was in 1640. The "Down Survey" is a listing of all of the forfeited lands after the Cromwellian victory. Both of these surveys have been published by the Irish Manuscripts Commission and are available in many large public and university libraries.
collection is in the PRO. Recently the name of the Public Record Office (PRO) has been changed to the National Archives of Ireland. The address is:

National Archives of Ireland-PRO
Four Courts Bldg.
Dublin, Republic of Ireland

Many other Irish records and much genealogical information in general from both the north and the south of Ireland can be had from:

The Chief Herald
Genealogical Office
Kildare Street
Dublin, Republic of Ireland

As mentioned earlier, the Registry of Deeds began in 1708. Therefore, it would not show any original deeds of the very earliest of the Scot planters, although it would show any later changes. The "Civil Survey 1654-56" is a listing of the proprietors of land at that time. It would be essentially the same as in the early part of that century. The "Down Survey" mentioned earlier is a listing of all of the forfeited lands after the Cromwellian victory and the names of the new owners. Both of these surveys have been published by the Irish Manuscript Commission and are available in many large public and university libraries.

The "Books of Survey and Distribution" record the proprietors in 1670, that is, after the transplantation to Connaught and Clare of the original Irish and Anglo-Irish land owners. Four of the volumes of this work have also been published by the Irish Manuscripts Commission.

There are a considerable number of Plantation Records available in the PRO in Dublin and the PRONI in Belfast. The book mentioned earlier by George Hill, "An Historical Account of the Plantation of Ulster, 1608-1620" provides a great deal of detailed information concerning original settlers. It is available in both the PRO and PRONI. A reprint has been available from the Irish University Press in Dublin. "The Journal of the Armagh Diocesan Historical Society" in the PRONI also contains many old records as does "Ulster Inquisitions".

A number of genealogical societies have been formed in recent years in Northern Ireland. As in England they are known as Family History Societies. If you would like to know if there is such a society in your area of interest in Northern Ireland, write to:

Rev. H. Kelso
67 Marlborough Park, South
Belfast, NORTHERN IRELAND U.K.

Please enclose one or two International Reply Coupons instead of the usual SASE.

The Linen Hall Library has a large collection of early newspapers. The obituary, birth and marriage colums of these papers have been indexed. It also has a collection of over 700 family trees of families from Belfast, Co. Down and County Antrim, as well as a large number of published family histories. The address of this library is:

Linen Hall Library
Wellington Place
Belfast, 1, NORTHERN IRELAND U.K.

There are two good bookstores in Belfast which can supply books on various aspects of history or research. An inquiry to them with International Reply Coupons enclosed for return postage, should bring back a list of books and prices on any subject that you request. The two bookstores are:

Cathedral Book Store
18 Gresham Street
Belfast, NORTHERN IRELAND U.K.

University Bookshop, Ltd.
50 University Road
Belfast, NORTHERN IRELAND U.K.

Northern Ireland government publications may be obtained from:

Her Majesty's Stationery Office
Chichester Street
Belfast, NORTHERN IRELAND U.K.

One of the most important publications of this office is the "Report of the Deputy Keeper of the Public Record Office of Northern Ireland". This has been published irregularly in about 24 volumes since 1924. These list all of the records, books, manuscripts, etc. accumulated in the PRONI. The last three or four of such reports are usually still available from the above address at reasonable prices. An entire or partial collection of these can sometimes be obtained from bookstores. Make an enquiry to either place concerning price and availability. Many large libraries in the United States have some or the full series. These, too, can be obtained on Inter-Library Loan. These reports provide details on all of the thousands of documents available at the Public Record Office of Northern Ireland.

There are a number of bibliographic sources listing publications of all kinds for history and research in Ireland. The most comprehensive of these covering both the North and the South is Richard J. Hayes, "Manuscript Sources for the History of Irish Civilization",(11 volumes),Boston: G.K.Hall (1965). Also there is "Sources for the History of Irish Civilization: Articles in Periodicals", (9 volumes) by Richard J. Hayes, Boston: G.K. Hall(1970).

This book is not intended to be a guide to research in Scotland, even though that was the original home of the Scotch-Irish. SUMMIT PUBLCATIONS publishes another book, SCOTTISH FAMILY RESEARCH which discusses record sources in Scotland as well as other information for the Scottish researcher.

SUMMIT PUBLICATIONS

now published by

Ye Olde Genealogie Shoppe

PO Box 39128

Indianapolis, IN 46239

1-317-862-3330

GERMAN FAMILY RESEARCH MADE SIMPLE by J. Konrad - Revised 1992 - 108 pages $10.00

IRISH FAMILY RESEARCH MADE SIMPLE by E. J. Collins - Revised 1993 - 77 pages $8.00

SCOTCH-IRISH FAMILY RESEARCH MADE SIMPLE by R. G. Campbell - Revised 1992 - 65 pages $8.00

POLISH FAMILY RESEARCH by J. Konrad - Revised 1992 - 72 pages $8.00

ENGLISH FAMILY RESEARCH by J. Konrad - Revised 1989 - 65 pages $8.00

ITALIAN FAMILY RESEARCH by J. Konrad - Revised 1990 - 63 pages $8.00

FRENCH AND FRENCH-CANADIAN FAMILY RESEARCH by J. Konrad - Revised 1993 79 pages $8.00

MEXICAN AND SPANISH FAMILY RESEARCH by J. Konrad - First Edition 1989 - 70 pages $8.00

SCOTTISH FAMILY RESEARCH by J. Konrad - First Edition 1989 - 56 pages $8.00

DIRECTORY OF FAMILY "ONE-NAME" PERIODICALS edited by J. Konrad - 1992/1993 edition $8.00

FAMILY ASSOCIATIONS, SOCIETIES AND REUNIONS Edited by J. Konrad - 1992/1993 edition $8.00

GENEALOGICAL SOCIETIES & HISTORICAL SOCIETIES IN THE UNITED STATES edited by J. Konrad - 1992/1993 edition $8.00

Please add $3.00 shipping and handling charge per order.